1965

DRIVING FORCES IN HISTORY

DRIVING

Drivmakter i historia, Oslo, 1959
Translated from the
Norwegian by Einar Haugen

IN

HALVDAN

FORCES

HISTORY

KOHT

THE BELKNAP PRESS OF HARVARD UNIVERSITY PRESS
CAMBRIDGE, MASSACHUSETTS · 1964

FOREWORD

If I were called upon to name the dean of living historians, Halvdan Koht would immediately leap to my mind. This distinguished Norwegian scholar has passed his ninetieth year, from which impressive age he can look back not only on an exceptionally rich professional life, but also on a noteworthy career of public service. Historians quite rightly value government service as an adjunct to their academic work. Dr. Koht, as one of the leaders of the Norwegian Labor Party, served as his country's foreign minister from 1935 to 1941—heartbreaking years for all Europe, which for Norway culminated in Hitler's surprise invasion in April 1940. Historian Koht has seen more history in the making than most men would wish for.

Dr. Koht's professional career has been a truly eminent one. Though a citizen of one of the smaller countries, he had already achieved an international reputation when most of the senior members of the profession were only just getting started. For many years he served as the chairman of the International Committee of the Historical Sciences and was a familiar figure at all the international congresses. He was, in fact, very much an internationalist. Educated at German and French as well as at Scandinavian universities, he was professionally interested in the history of all European countries, not to say of the world, for he visited and taught in the United States on various occasions and wrote a book on the political and cultural impact of

America upon Europe. His whole conception of history was broad and generous, for he studied literary affairs with the same devotion as the political or the economic. The long list of his publications begins with a biography of Norway's great poet and champion of liberty, Henrik Wergeland, and includes one of the truly distinguished biographies of Henrik Ibsen.

The present volume embodies the reflections and the judgments of this great historian on some of the forces that have conditioned mankind's development. Dr. Koht's approach is that of a socialist. He is convinced, as he says, that what changes in time is not man, but the economic and social conditions in which at any period he has his being. But he is far too good a historian to believe that any one explanation will cover the problem. He fully recognizes the role which religion has played in human affairs and he is almost startlingly modern in his emphasis on the importance of psychological factors. The reader will find here a tribute to the pioneer efforts of William McDougall in the field of social psychology as well as to the impressive contributions of Freud to the understanding of human motivations. In his effort to establish the driving forces in historical development, Dr. Koht touches on many problems of current interest, such as class conflict, the changing nature and power of the state, the role of nationalism. His conclusions reflect the distillation of a long lifetime of study and experience in public affairs. This is a book marked not only by searching analysis, but by wisdom and deep human understanding. It will richly reward anyone concerned with mankind and the vicissitudes of human society.

WILLIAM L. LANGER

Harvard University
February 22, 1964

CONTENTS

FOREWORD BY WILLIAM L. LANGER   v

AUTHOR'S PREFACE   ix

I   WHAT IS IT THAT CHANGES IN HISTORY?   1

II   CAUSES IN HISTORY   24

III   RELIGION AS A SOCIAL FORCE   32

IV   THE SPIRIT OF COOPERATION IN STATE AND NATION   58

V   ECONOMIC FORCES   82

VI   CLASS CONSCIOUSNESS   106

VII   REVOLT AND OBEDIENCE   123

VIII   THE ADVANCING POWER OF THE STATE   137

IX   WAR AS A DESTROYER AND A STIMULUS   153

X   SCIENCE AS A FORCE IN SOCIETY   163

XI   INFLUENCE AMONG NATIONS   174

XII   INTERNATIONALISM   189

XIII   CONCLUSION   201

NOTES   207

INDEX   211

PREFACE

This book does not attempt to present a philosophy of history, if only for the reason that its author is not a philosopher, but a historian. This does not mean that I would wish to ban philosophizing from history, any more than from life. In one fashion or another we must all shape for ourselves a philosophy of life, and this must include history as surely as there is a bond between the past and the present. But I am inclined to say with one of Pasternak's characters: "In my opinion, philosophy should be a spice to be taken only in small doses, as a supplement to life and art."

Anyone who works with history will often find himself pondering on the causes of the events he encounters there. In my long life I have strayed into many areas of historical activity. So it is only natural that more than thirty years ago I began to make plans for fitting all my special researches into a wider perspective. In so doing I have remained on purely historical ground. By this I mean that I reason about history on the basis of facts. And I use only such facts as I know from more or less independent research, facts which I therefore think I can venture to build on with some confidence. As testimony of this I have now and then throughout the book referred to those of my writings in which I have embodied the results of my researches. In some cases I have also indicated how I arrived at my opinions on particular problems. In this way the book has acquired a strongly personal coloring. This may give a certain insight into the way in which a historian—or at least one historian—works and thinks.

H. K.

For the English translation it seems appropriate to add that the original plan for this book was developed in the fall semester of 1930 when I was a visiting professor at Harvard University and gave a graduate course on this topic. The discussions with my students were of great assistance in clarifying the problems for me.

June 1963

DRIVING FORCES IN HISTORY

Chapter I

WHAT IS IT THAT CHANGES IN HISTORY?

At the International Congress of Historians in Zürich in 1938 the Rumanian historian Nicolae Jorga gave a paper on what he called *les permanences de l'histoire*—the constants of historical change. Jorga was a witty man, though not a particularly original thinker, and the things he had to say about his theme were therefore not new, but he expressed them in a thought-provoking way. He wished to emphasize the importance of physiographical conditions in the history of man. As examples he mentioned, among others, the ores that gave rise to mining and created a Bronze Age and an Iron Age, and the sea that made coastal peoples like the Norwegians into sailors.

While he spoke, I could not help thinking that all of these natural resources could have no consequences for history until man had learned to exploit them. The ore had no influence until men mastered the art of smelting, nor the sea until they learned how to sail it. I therefore got up and said that the one and only "permanence" in history was man himself. He was so not only because he was the proper theme of history, but also because he was the greatest force in historical development. And he was an enduring force because throughout history he remained "permanent," motivated by the same mental traits and making use of the same abilities.

The mode of thinking that underlay my contribution was based on what I had learned of modern psychological research, particularly the study of man in society. The pioneering work here was William McDougall's *Introduction to Social Psychology*, the first edition of which appeared in 1908. Then there was his later work, *The Group Mind* (1920), where he attempted to utilize social psychology to explain historical change. I was not as happy about his later book, for he often did not get beneath the surfaces of history or beyond elementary schoolbook knowledge, and therefore failed to plumb the depths of the mental life that he was studying. But such reservations could not overturn Mc-Dougall's basic idea, his doctrine of the enduring psychological motivation of man.

There had been various impulses in earlier research that pointed toward this approach. I am not now thinking of the facile talk by so many historians, both earlier and later, about "national character" or "racial traits" and that sort of thing. Most of this was based more on speculation than on genuine research. The pioneering thinkers of the eighteenth century, especially a man like Montesquieu, were looking for an explanation of the peculiar temperament they thought they had discovered among primitive peoples. They found it in the climate and other natural conditions which they thought could influence psychology in various ways. Of those who asserted these views, surely no one did so with a more severely logical consistency than the positivist Buckle in the 1850's and 1860's. He even assumed that historical environment could give rise to specific traits, for example, the religious fanaticism of the Spaniards.

I was to some extent influenced by this doctrine when I wrote my paper in 1905 entitled "Backgrounds of Norwegian Politics."[1] In this study I tried to demonstrate how social and economic conditions from the sixteenth to the eighteenth century had created a mentality among Norwegian farmers (*bønder*) that gave rise to the agrarian political movement of the nineteenth century. But here there was no question of basic traits of character, only of particular shapes or expressions of universal psychological traits and tendencies, so that in this respect I was more in harmony with recent psychology. Nor did I base my argument on speculation but on the concrete expression of thoughts and feelings to be found in folklore and poetry. My attempt was to write history from the point of view of psychology.

At this time Gustave Le Bon had also made his bold proposal to shape a science out of previous speculation in the works he wrote in the 1890's concerning "mass psychology." They aroused a great deal of controversy and discussion, because they seriously raised the question of whether it was possible to speak of a collective psychology. Here McDougall made his contribution by penetrating to the deepest urges of all human beings and pointing out how these urges constantly lived and had power in human society through all changes in external conditions. These ideas gave new perspectives on the past as well as the future and required a new explanation of historical change.

In the half century that has passed since that time, social psychology has made great strides. Above all, we can thank Freud and psychoanalysis for many new insights. Historical scholarship cannot remain uninfluenced by our new awareness of the vast importance for humanity of the milieu, the social environment, even from early childhood. But the crucial point in all of this is that the psychological traits and capacities of man have constantly remained the same.

Even McDougall, when he looked back on history, could be assailed by doubts. He felt he had to take up once more the old question of whether acquired traits and abilities could be inherited. He made experiments with animals (mice) having particularly rapid changes of generation. Once (in 1930) I had the opportunity myself of watching some of his experiments. But the results were completely negative. One could only be left with the conviction that the basic traits of man had maintained themselves as constants through all time. Even the latest Russian researches have not been able to shake this idea.

The race of man has lived on earth for half a million or perhaps a million years. We might not wish to acknowledge the first man if we met him today, whether he came from the innermost part of Asia or from South Africa or from western Europe. That low forehead, that jutting jawbone— it would all remind us more of an animal than of a man. Perhaps the anthropologists can establish that there once were men who did not have as intricate brains or such multipurpose limbs as we have today. Differing mutations may have created differing forms of man. We are still deplorably uninformed about the racial history of man, the story of how men have been transformed into the shape we know today.

We know equally little about the lengthy, tortuous, and difficult task of cultivation that led man forward to the cultural level he had reached when he finally stepped into the historical limelight some ten or twenty thousand years ago. All our sciences—psychology and sociology, ethnography and archeology—give us meager assistance in pursuing man from one little cultural advance to the next. Perhaps a man of letters like Johannes V. Jensen, the Danish author of *The Long Journey*, can teach us more than any scientist about the way in which the first men found the tools and the strength to defend life against wild beasts and other dangers, and how they joined together into societies in the struggle for existence. Most of this took place prior to everything we call history, even if we include our knowledge of what we call prehistory.

The history we know, though only through scattered glimpses in its earliest phases, is associated with people who by their anthropological structure are members of the same races that sustain culture in our day also. We cannot point out any basic difference between the peoples now living and those whose remains we find in ancient Assyria or Egypt, China or India, Greece or Italy. These races may be somewhat unlike in various parts of the earth. Yet their basic traits, physical or psychological, their willpower and their abilities, were surely the same in all, even if some may have been more or less highly developed, as is also the case among individuals today.

Even if we can now maintain this idea, nothing is more certain than that the basic traits are not permitted to express themselves in the same way in all periods of life on earth. We hear endless tales about violence and barbarity in ancient times that repel us strongly. These are not merely individual instances, but practices that were once universal—violence towards women, vengeance on enemies, torturing and branding as punishment for crimes. The individuals also seem to us to have been wilder, more unrestrained in their emotional life. We are startled at the horrible terms of abuse that even highly cultivated people could direct at one another, and at the way in which they could let themselves be possessed by anger. I recall how it struck me as something from a completely alien age when I read that the honorable old *statholder* of Schleswig-Holstein, Henrik Rantzau, in the year 1593 became so angry at a court session that his whole body shook. Two of his fingers were paralyzed and immovable because of his anger; he cried out loud and ran from the courtroom. We could hardly imagine anything like this happening in our culture a mere three centuries later.

Even though the tendencies are the same, the restraints are in many fields much stronger today. Social life has created mechanisms that keep the instincts from finding free expression, so that they are subject to sublimation. Restraints have been imposed by training and teaching at home and in school from childhood on, by submission to custom and law, in a more and more complex cooperation with others.

We have been taught to smile at Socrates for being so naive that he thought people would do what was right and good if only they knew what it was. But history has shown us quite clearly that we must not be so pessimistic as to think that knowledge and teaching do nothing for human progress. It is society that teaches us to restrain ourselves. Only people with inferior or distorted psychological abilities will not let themselves be restrained in this way, people who can easily become violators of the laws of society. There may be quite unusual circumstances that loose the bonds of society and remove the inhibitions on the instincts. But the normal thing today is that people control their instincts, or at least control them a great deal more than in former times.

This is the way with many other phenomena from olden times that now seem strange to us. We may encounter a religion or a morality deviating so strongly from our own that we cannot without the greatest difficulty seize the ideas and feelings underlying a mode of thought that once was universal. I remember witnessing in my youth (in 1895) the divine services of Arabian dervishes in Constantinople, both the "howling" and the "whirling" kinds. I saw how they swayed their bodies back and forth as they sat by the hour repeating the same monotonous cry, *il Allah il Allah*, or how they whirled around and around until they collapsed. In both cases the goal was to attain such ecstasy that they might think they were meeting God. This behavior was to me so strange, so much a heritage of primitive times, that it seemed quite incomprehensible. Not until much later, through researches in religious history, did I learn that these actions were special expressions of instincts and tendencies that live in us to this very day. Now as always, man loves and fears, feels desire and repulsion, has a need to obey or a will to rebel, a desire to gather in flocks or to battle his fellows. The only things that change are the factors that condition the forms assumed by such instincts and traits and their infinitely varied interplay.

The unbroken continuity of human life struck me most vividly when I was traveling in Southern Italy and Sicily in 1925. Here were such abundant memorials from many older cultures, Greek, Roman, Arabic, and Norman. This was ancient soil, where men had labored to create the values of life through thousands upon thousands of years. What there made the new any different from the old? The thing that moved me more profoundly than anything else I saw was the endless care that had been devoted to making the soil fruitful. Up and down the stony hills, in every tiny nook or cranny, people had shown their will to work. Stone was laid upon stone, building one wall above the other. The hills were transformed into row upon row of fields filled with good, fruitful soil, which was tended and cared for. No doubt there had been changes down through time in the plants that were cultivated. It was surely rather new for cactus figs and lemon trees to occupy so much space. There must have been a time when olive trees and grape-vines were new plants as well, but even this was already some two thousand years ago. And what difference did it really make whether people found one tree or another most profitable? The effort put forth and the manner of labor had always been much the same. Almost endlessly far back men must have been busied in preparing these hills in the same way, thinking about how they should bind the earth, stamping it down, and digging in it. Stone-paved roads and paths winding up the hills were surely the same today as they were a thousand or two thousand years ago.

Then I went to see the past in the museum at Syracuse. On the street outside I passed a mother who was carrying her child, carefully wrapped inside her black shawl. Inside the museum I found myself in front of a little Greek figurine in terra cotta, more than two thousand years old. Trait by trait it was the Syracusan mother I had seen outside. Not only was the mother love the same, but her dress as well, and the whole characteristic manner in which she carried her child. It was all like a portrait of today. In the museum I found prehistoric agricultural implements that were the counterparts of those I saw in use in the fields today. And I saw that people still made jugs for wine and water in the same shapes as those of prehistoric times.

Working life and customs were not the only things that remained the same. Did not in reality these people live in the same way as their ancestors had through all the ages? Then as now, they must have been building their houses of the same material, of the yellowish-white limestone that they joined with earth or clay dried in the sun. And they built their dwellings according to the same basic plan, not to live in, but to sleep in—deep, dark rooms facing on deep, narrow streets. I imagine that the villages of Greek and Roman times made much the same impression as those one can see now in that country—white spots among the hills, where people live closely packed, where they fill the streets with their bustle, and do their work on the hills around the village.

In spite of all the monuments of the past that might seem so different, Greek temples or Roman amphitheaters, I could not shake off the feeling that here men still lived in the ancient mold. Their minds were filled with the same thoughts. They toiled and pondered, jested and sorrowed in essentially the same way. In recent years they had gotten electric light into their murky cellars. But one could not see that they had changed their behavior or their character to any noticeable extent. Had all these thousand years gone over their heads without a trace? Even though they now attended Christian churches, crossed themselves before sacred images and splashed holy water on themselves, it is not certain that their feelings were any different from what they had been when they went to pagan temples, bent their knees to the gods, and sacrificed the meat of animals. Travel in such a country as this gives one an overwhelming sense of how conservative life can be, of how the present vividly reflects the past. And this applies more strongly to man's psychology than to anything else.

Now it is true that research in prehistory teaches us a great deal about the stubbornness with which men could maintain their use of tools and their customs through thousands upon thousands of years, so that much that is old could survive many kinds of change. And in many places more or less primitive societies have been able to survive down to our own day. But it is still true, as Henry Adams so strongly emphasized in his historical philosophy, that in the most advanced societies change and transformation are taking place at a constantly increasing rate. In the last two or three generations so much has changed that we sometimes feel the world around us has been completely reshaped before our eyes. If we look back only a few centuries, we are given pause by deeds that look as if they were expressions of a completely different emotional life among men.

There is scarcely anything that strikes us so forcibly as the contrast between the hard-bitten cruelty we hear about in the Middle Ages or even some centuries later, and the gentleness of heart that now alone seems worthy to be called human. We shudder quite involuntarily when we read about the monstrous tortures people at that time could inflict on one another, the maiming of the body that they could perform with such wild delight. We can hardly bear to think of anything so frightful. I know that for a long time I went around asking myself if this was not evidence that we had become better people, milder in our very emotions, endowed with other urges in our soul, with greater capacities for sympathy than our ancestors had had, with a more abundant will to help our weak and infirm fellow beings.

But the events of the World War of 1914 taught me that the merciless will to torture other people still could rise up in all its terror. And the unspeakable horrors that the Nazis only two decades later could let loose on an old land of culture like Germany put an end to any idea I might have had about a possible change in the human heart. For that matter I could have recalled how Christians in my own country condemned people whose beliefs differed from theirs to eternal suffering in hell—though I had noticed that people were beginning to talk less and less about hell.

No, I had to face the fact that if any change had occurred,

it was due to a more or less universal advance in man's fellow-feeling, an expansion of his capacity for compassion with suffering. In other words, ancient human traits had won greater strength, in step with a social change, a reinforcement of social life that checked evil-doing and provided better opportunities for the natural urge to help. In the depths of our souls we were no better than we ever had been.

Some may say that in the course of time men have become wiser and more clever, that their capacity for thinking has been refined and enriched. Would it have been possible four or five thousand years ago to teach people all the thoughts we can now juggle in mathematics or philosophy, for example? Even in our day there is great variation in the capacity of different people and different races in this respect. Many say that at least some "low" layers of society can never manage to assimilate the highest ideas of culture as their own. But then it will happen that even among such retarded and perhaps ungifted peoples a man arises who in one leap reaches the highest summits of human thought. Then one must ask if it was not after all the external opportunities that were lacking, not the intellectual capacities. As far as our own Germanic ancestors are concerned, one would suppose that at least their brain capacity was no different from ours. It was scarcely a difference in inborn talent that made it possible for a Greek philosopher twenty-five hundred years ago to think thoughts that would have been quite inscrutable to a Germanic barbarian of his time.

Even though we have vaulted to previously unknown heights of thinking, the truth unquestionably is that it took at least as great a genius and just as intense mental activity to think the first thoughts or make the first inventions that gave us the bases of human culture. The leap which the man of culture makes from the elements of physics or chemistry to the most intricate technical inventions, or from historical and biological learning to comprehensive thinking about universal laws of life—this leap is no greater than the one which primitive man had to make from his straight-forward struggle for existence to the oldest, roughhewn implements of stone, or to such an artful instrument as the wheel, or from terror at the forces of nature to the concept of a divine will.

We who are alive today inherit without excessive effort an endless array of intellectual instruments that generations have fashioned for us through the millennia. It is not our own gifts that have grown and placed us on a higher level. We build on circumstances our ancestors lacked, but which they have conferred upon us. We belong to a society with long roots back into the past, and it is this society that preserves and protects for us all that the preceding generations have won.

Wherever we turn and however we ask the question, we always get this answer, that what changes in history is not man himself, but the circumstances on which he builds, the society in which he lives. History is therefore not the story of individuals, but of society and changes in society. The individual gains his significance for history only by the activity he performs in society and by the effect which society has on him. Even this is saying a great deal.

It is no novel concept to say that history is primarily social history. As far as I know, this was first advanced and sustained by Condorcet, one of the men of the eighteenth-century Enlightenment, who participated in the French Revolution. In the last year of his life (1794), proscribed by his own revolution, he wrote his chief work, a survey of the intellectual history of mankind. His purpose was to portray the transformation of common ways of thinking in

knowledge and in morality. He knew well that individuals
had their place in this history. There could be priests and
tyrants who checked the progress of intellect and freedom,
or there could be lawmakers and thinkers, especially
scientists, who promoted enlightenment, intellectual and
political liberation. But it was an error of historians, he said,
to make these individuals the main theme of their works.
True history concerned those who in truth were the race
of man, the great mass that constituted society and maintained it with their work.

This outlook was first adopted and defended in Norway
by the poet Henrik Wergeland in his remarkable treatise
of 1843, "The Result of History." In this he wrote that the
cultural status of a people should not be judged by "the
individual geniuses or the accomplishments in art and
science" of which it could boast, but by the place these
occupied in their social life. History should accordingly
judge in this way: "Just as it is not the birth of Homer or
Phidias or Plato, but their general cultivation which gives
the Greeks a position of preeminence in the history of
ancient culture, so it is not the names of Newton or Davy,
but the fructification of their genius, the practical acquaint-
ance of the masses with their discoveries, which gives the
English their precedence among cultured nations."

What interested Condorcet as well as Wergeland and all
their contemporaries in this history of society, was *progress*.
He and the others could easily perceive many reactions
and defeats in the struggle for intellectual advancement, for
justice and truth. Only a few years earlier Gibbon had
given the world his powerful depiction of the fall of the
great Roman Empire, so that it had to be clear to everyone
that history was not just progress. But the human spirit
had constantly been gaining victories, and through the
great revolutions in America and France it had had a final

breakthrough that promised new, continual, and unlimited progress. For the enlightenment of the eighteenth century, said Condorcet, had advanced a new idea that put an end to all old prejudices. This was the idea of the illimitable perfectibility of man. In the light of this he envisaged a tremendous advance, which in the end would unite all the peoples of earth in a great society of universal enlightenment.

In this way Condorcet laid the scientific, historical foundation for the faith in progress that was going to infuse the whole nineteenth century. He imagined that the new conditions to be created by discoveries in science and art and by a growing general prosperity would bring about also a perfection of the intellectual and moral capacities of men. But it is worth while here to keep clearly in mind that he did not speak of any kind of transmutation or reshaping of the inborn traits. What he meant was that the intellect would have the opportunity of working with a far richer supply of knowledge. And he emphasized that the new "moral goodness" would be a social product based on a more equitable legal system and a universal humanity.

It is obvious enough when we look back on human history from the vantage point of our own day that there has been enormous progress. For philosophers of history it was inevitably tempting to concentrate on this general progress. Thinkers as different as Hegel and Comte were alike in regarding history as a kind of logical idea put into practice: one intellectual link followed naturally upon another. Such an intellectual construct appears tremendously impressive. But living history has a wealth of material in it that can not be locked up in rigid schemes. We are forced to follow history through all kinds of changing movements and explore in it all the forces that affect the life of man. For this reason historians of the twentieth century have more and more given up the word "progress" and have exchanged it for the more neutral word "change."

No matter how much one may agree that "the world advances," one still discovers rather quickly that every forward step has its drawback. It is at least an old complaint that various good things are lost precisely because of progress. The old patriarchal bond between worker and employer was shattered in modern industry. The cozy twilight hour in the inglenook was dispelled by the kerosene lamp and the electric light. Many have feared that "the welfare state" will put an end to individual initiative. Henrik Ibsen bewailed that "Herr von Moltke murdered the poetry of battle" by his "state machinery," and others have maintained that with modern weapons all "heroic" virtues have vanished. Just the same there are few people in a cultured society who wish their states to get involved in a war. Condorcet remarked about heroism that there is abundant use for it in many other fields beside war.

A more significant criticism of the idea of universal progress is the fact that it does not apply equally to all kinds of cultural endeavor. A people may be highly advanced in one aspect of culture and lag far behind in another. We dare not say that we have in all respects advanced beyond older peoples. This is particularly clear in the field of art. To find the high point in dramatic art, we have to go three hundred and fifty years back to the great master, Shakespeare—perhaps even to the Greek tragedians of nearly twenty-five hundred years ago. One of the greatest compliments that could be paid to Ibsen was to say that his dramas were reminiscent of the ancient Greek tragedies. In sculpture, the Greeks still have pride of place. In painting, the Renaissance is still the greatest flowering. If we turn from Europe to Asia, we find the high point of Chinese art in much older ages. So it goes in one area after the other in the history of art and literature.

Even in other forms of life one can find parallels to such alternations of progress and reaction. When at the International Congress of Historians at Brussels in 1923 the Belgian historian Henri Pirenne gave a lecture on the underlying trends in economic history, he pointed out the remarkable oscillation between freedom and regulation over the last millennium and a half. In the early centuries of the Middle Ages all economic life was bound in traditional forms, down to the resumption of trade in the twelfth century. Then followed a new restriction through the guilds in the fourteenth and fifteenth centuries, and a new freedom with the Renaissance and dawning capitalism in the sixteenth century. The mercantilism of the seventeenth and eighteenth centuries brought with it state regulation, which was relaxed by the tremendous breakthrough of industrial capitalism and liberalism in the nineteenth century, followed by new state regulation through socialism in the twentieth. Pirenne himself did not venture to say that there was a historical law in this oscillation; he only wanted to raise the question. For my own part I feel it is impossible to make any kind of a law out of it. For there was so great an unlikeness in the forms of economic freedom and economic restriction and in the conditions that had created them that the similarities were largely superficial. The oscillation could become a law only if it were demonstrated that the change from one form to the other arose from a natural reaction against the prevailing one, a reaction which then had to lead society over to the opposite extreme. In reality, I held, each change represented the appearance of new social forces, and I would not accept the idea of a regular alternation.

A much more searching attack on the faith in inevitable progress in history was the one Oswald Spengler made in his book *Der Untergang des Abendlandes* ("The Decline of the West"), which appeared in two volumes in 1918 and 1922. It was a vigorous attempt to provide a scientific basis for a feeling that time and again had overcome people who thought they saw decline and decadence around them—a feeling that the people or the society to which they belonged had become too old and was facing its end. Spengler believed that this was the case with the entire social order of the West. He found a law in it, because he thought he saw parallels to it in older social orders. In his eyes the history of the world was a never-ending alternation between different forms of culture. Each culture, he believed, had its particular stamp, its own soul and spirit, and when this particular soul had attained its perfection, it lost its creative capacity, and the culture of which it was born had to die. Within each form of culture, history became a story of budding, blossoming, and withering.

Spengler tried to establish this for three distinct cultures —the Byzantine, the Greco-Roman, and the modern Western culture. He did it with spirit and broad perspective, and he had a great many instructive things to say about the historical periods he discussed. I will not go into any of that. The main point of interest here is his doctrine of the distinct cultures into which he split the history of the world. This doctrine was again taken up in an even wider perspective by Arnold J. Toynbee in his great work, *A Study of History*, which began appearing in 1934 and was completed with its tenth volume in 1954. He encompassed the history of the whole world, not just of Europe, and he split it up into a round score of distinct cultures which all had in common the fact that they blossomed and died.

Yet his conclusion was quite different from Spengler's. This was due to the fact that while Spengler looked on the destruction of each culture as something inevitable, against which men might struggle in vain, Toynbee believed in the human will as a major force in cultural life.

When Spengler contemplated his own age, he thought he saw that it had lost precisely that capacity for creation that has to be the central force in cultural growth. There was an end, he felt, to all new poetry, all new art, all new science. Now it was the engineers, the factory, that had made themselves the masters of society and were giving free rein to the predatory instincts of man. Violence and dictatorships would mark the last phases of Western culture, just as they had in the Roman Empire. A new culture would emerge and become the dawn of a new age. He believed that this was getting under way in Russia.

In some respects one can say that Spengler prophesied correctly or almost correctly. Technical inventions have given rise to vast reshapings of social life and at the same time threaten to destroy it completely. Many may think they see the future in Russia. He believed that the creative spirit in Western culture was dead, but we dare surely say now that he was mistaken. He who himself was a mathematician believed that no renewal was possible in mathematics, but he forgot that Einstein was at work on just such a renewal. He thought that the science of history had buried itself in detailed research and lost the capacity of making large syntheses, but he was himself providing testimony to the continual vitality of this spirit. A further straw in the wind was the extensive controversy that his doctrine aroused among historians and laymen the world around.

Toynbee started from the same premise as Spengler, but

he found reason to hope that occidental culture might still be able to renew itself. He pinned his hopes on religion. Sometimes he would speak as if he thought Christianity could save our culture. But if his ideas were to have any meaning whatever, it had to be the universal religious urge in man, his faith in the powers of life, his confidence in the strength of life in all of us, which would guide us to new advances.

In making an exception of the occidental culture that Spengler had condemned to death, Toynbee in reality gave up the doctrine of a continual alternation in history among distinct and independent cultures. For myself I can only say that the whole idea seems artificial, out of touch with the realities of life. I see in history much more of a living continuity.

Perhaps it is possible to say with some justice that Chinese history does show such a repeated downfall and renewal that we can speak of a series of distinct cultural periods, for in that country the continuity was broken by barbaric invaders from the outside. But something of the old still maintained itself through all interruptions, so that the new could build upon it.

The most drastic interruption we know in any cultural development was probably the one that occurred when the European conquistadors came and destroyed the culture of the Aztecs and the Incas. But this is a special case and cannot be made the basis of a general historical theory.

If we confine ourselves just to that which leads forward to European culture as it is today, we will find its roots far back in time and in many countries. Egyptian, Assyrian, Phoenician, and Cyprian cultures all figure among the antecedents of Greek culture. From Greece the path leads forward both to Roman and to Christian culture. We in our time have a precious freight of both Greek and Roman heritage. Indic and Chinese culture have not always lived by themselves and are today in the midst of a great renewal. One can no doubt say the same about Islam. Even if the world was once divided, there has always been growing cooperation. Continuity is more important in history than division.

Besides, it is a great mistake to conceive each culture as a kind of self-contained world. It is true enough that in ancient times the social environment had greater power over the individual than it usually has today. But individuals have always and everywhere been able to break through their environment. Spengler even regarded it as a special trait of occidental culture that it had what he called the "Faustian" spirit, filled with internal strife and contradictions. Thereby he put his finger on something dynamic that automatically bursts the bonds of the culture and gives rise to renewal and innovation.

Even if some cultures have had to founder and have not been permitted to grow and expand on their own former base, one can find a natural explanation for this in other ways. Henrik Wergeland observed that social circumstances form the background of the destruction of older cultures as well as the bright hope of our own. In the above-mentioned paper, "The Result of History," his basic thesis was that all cultural effort has a continuation, even if the people that makes it is subjugated or destroyed. He then goes on:

The farther back we go in time, the more conspicuous is the difference in the distribution of culture among peoples. Hence the total disappearance of so many that have scintillated in history. Carthage with its noble families vanished like the faithless Syrte, and the proud people of Rome did not survive its patricians. But our age has come to realize that the basis of happiness and survival for a people is a universal culture, and that without this the efforts of the individual are but insecure.

This is to say that a purely upper-class culture is doomed to destruction, while a broad culture for the whole people produces the conditions for ever-new advances. And this is because ever-new families then can rise up and enter the work of culture with fresh abilities.

In fact, the idea that cultures or people could age and therefore have to die was an extrapolation from natural science to social history. It was imagined that human society had to have the same fate as the individual person. This completely naive idea appeared to gain scientific support as natural science won more and more dominance over men's thinking. Society came to be looked on as an organism, subject to the biological laws that applied to all organic life. This view was shaped primarily by Herbert Spencer, and it was in a form that could easily capture the imagination. There were many analogies, such as the differentiation that constantly created new species, or the atrophy that made formerly useful organs into obstacles to progress. It was not noticed that all such analogies in reality were nothing but metaphors to assist our understanding. They did not mean true identity.

Henry Adams played with the idea a half-century ago that some day it would be possible to express all historic change in mathematical formulas like those Newton and Gibbs had invented, and to make them the laws of history. But he was quite aware of the fact that these were metaphors drawn from natural science. The great atomic physicist Niels Bohr more recently proposed to apply laws from his science in biology and psychology, but he did not go beyond the individual human being. He did not try to apply them to the society man has created around himself, for here it is not a question of atomic particles but of spiritual continuity. A whole society cannot be an organism in a biological sense. It is a union of a multitude of distinct organisms, people who individually and severally live and die according to biological laws. A society always renews itself as long as new people are born in it. Of course the new people inherit their forefathers, but they are not identical with them. They always bring something new into society. For this reason it is in reality meaningless to say that a culture or a nation grows "old" or is reduced in its energies as the years pass. On the contrary, a culture or a nation always has the strength of youth within it, and conditions quite different from age compel it to wither or to die.

Even though I do not, therefore, accept the attempts that have been made to substitute other causes of change in cultural history for the idea of progress, this does not of course mean that I believe all change to be identical with progress. We have too many evidences of retrogression or stagnation to believe anything like that. But we can safely assert that in all the countries of the earth there has been an observable progress away from a wholly primitive life. In historic time we can scarcely point to any people as truly primitive, living as man had to live when he first came into existence on this earth. If nothing else, men have acquired the skill of working with tools that demand both reflection and practice. They have scanned the skies to study the movements of the sun, the moon, and the stars. They have created for themselves both religious and magic concepts. They have responded to that need for cooperation which is the basis of all social life, and they have made for themselves many kinds of laws to regulate their intercourse. In most places of the earth the peoples have gone much farther and have departed even more from the life of the primitives.

If we look back on history from our present age, we can have no doubt that progress has been tremendous.

Progress has never been constant, however, and therefore we cannot expect constant progress in the days to come. I recall hearing in 1897 the historian Karl Lamprecht illustrate his conception of progress by drawing a line that slanted upward like a hill. But then he drew on the hill a long series of large and small humps, including some that were even higher than the point at which we were now standing. Such cultural peaks may occur in many specific areas, but general progress does not issue from the peaks. It comes from the foot of the peaks. In this way we make our way up the mountain step by step.

We cannot, however, be satisfied with this insight. It is necessary for us to investigate and clarify as far as we can the driving forces that impel men forward and thereby shape history.

Chapter II

CAUSES IN HISTORY

Man has always inquired about the causes of everything that happens to him and around him. It took a long time, however, before he began to glimpse the connection among all these events. His first idea was presumably that there were forces outside him that governed everything according to their will. To these forces he gave names. In this way he was able to make out a kind of continuity in life. He saw that the supernatural powers, at least those that governed nature, in some respects followed certain rules, as in the case of the changing sun and moon. In other respects things were pretty arbitrary. Wind and weather might change in many different ways, and in human life itself there was much that man was unable to master. He lived in a world of marvels, only he himself would not have called them marvels, for everything that differed from what he was accustomed to was still natural enough. The supernatural was the truly natural.

Even today we have to admit that human life is to a great degree subject to the same natural forces. The great scientist Wilhelm Ostwald believed that the true content of cultural progress was man's ability to master nature, his ability to subject the earth and all its forces to his own will. But we are still unable to master wind and weather. We cannot help it that the climate changes, giving abundance one year and drought the next, or that cod and herring come to land in great or little schools, and even move from one country to another. This and much else we are compelled to let nature decide.

In primitive ages people were perhaps even less willing than we to let nature remain an independent force unconnected with man and society. They preferred to believe that everything in nature was directed at man. When they saw a comet, they were frightened by this miraculous thing, and the tail of the comet appeared to them as a rod of punishment, a sign that God or the gods were angry at men for some crime they had committed. Similarly, all kinds of illness, especially great epidemics, could be regarded as punishment by supernatural powers. In this way they found a continuity in life, a causal connection in everything that occurred.

This primitive mode of thinking has in reality maintained itself down to our own time. It has taken the form of a faith that God rules everything, great as well as small. In my childhood I read (in a collection called "Christian Stories" by a Danish minister) a story about a man who blasphemously declared, "There is no God." Then he went out in the fields where a bolt of lightning flashed out from a clear sky and killed him. This was God's punishment.

This way of thinking has no place in the writing of history. But even if we do not wish to fit natural events into this kind of connection with human life, we still do not believe that nature determines historical events in a completely unconditional way. We will always ask what kind of conditions these events meet in human society. The conditions in society will determine the effect of the natural events. In each instance the question is how man can cope with the consequences of natural events, how he can resist misfortune or make use of its benefits. Arnold Toynbee made this into the great question of history—the basic law in human progress or regression, what he called the interplay between the "challenge" on the one side, and the human "response" on the other.

I question very much whether one can transform history into a struggle between man and nature. Nevertheless this is an important aspect of human life. It is obvious enough that men have gradually learned to make themselves more and more independent of nature. One or two thousand years ago a change of climate could determine whether people would survive and live comfortably in their country, or whether they had to migrate elsewhere. In our time it would take an extraordinary catastrophe before anything like this could take place.

There are many other factors that have their effect on social life and may appear to determine the course of history without any kind of assistance from us. The French philosopher Pascal once said that if Cleopatra's nose had been shorter, the whole face of the earth would have been changed. One might easily suppose he meant that it was a matter of pure chance that she got a lover who for her sake allowed Augustus to become master of the Roman Empire. This was not what Pascal meant by his jest. He merely wanted to point out that every little circumstance had its place in the chain of causes that constitutes history. Yet it does seem to have been a matter of chance just how Cleopatra's nose was shaped, or in other words whether or not she was a beautiful, seductive woman. There are many questions even greater than this which can lead us to think that pure chance has a tremendously decisive influence in history.

Let us consider an example from the history of Norway. In the last centuries of the Middle Ages it happened that one after another of the noble families died out. Either the last man of the family died childless, or he left only daughters as heirs. Then Danish or Swedish noblemen came to the country and took up the heritage after them. No native nobility remained to defend the independence of Norway. We do not know the biological laws that caused this fatal change in families. It looks to us like pure chance. We *can* say, however, that even before this the Norwegian nobility was on its way to being denationalized for other reasons. It was continually forming alliances with the Danish and Swedish nobility in a struggle for common class interests. If the nobility had not done this, its heritage would have fallen into Norwegian hands. Its property would have gone to men who could have risen into the nobility from other layers of society. We might conclude that under these circumstances Norway would have lost her independence in any event. We must grant, however, that this is a purely hypothetical statement and cannot be proved. The long series of deaths in the noble families was at least partially instrumental in determining the historical result.

Now in history it is quite possible that different causal chains may happen to cross one another at some point. We should then rather speak of coincidence than of pure chance. It may look like mere chance from one point of view, but on the other hand it may also appear as a natural consequence of well-known events. When the Spaniards discovered Mexico, subjugated the country, and enslaved the inhabitants, the connection with the general movement of European exploration is clear to us. To the Mexicans, however, it could only look like an unpredictable interruption of their history, something for which they could see no reason. The case will be the same if modern technicians succeed in landing on the moon. To us this will represent a continuation of diligent scientific efforts and experimentation. If we should find any kind of people on the moon, however, we would quite literally overwhelm them, like lightning from a clear sky. History abounds in what I have here called "coincidence," and historians have always taken it into account. One of the most eminent historical thinkers of antiquity, the Greek Polybius, often used the word "luck" (*túchē*) when he was going to tell about unexpected events. In modern times no less a historian than Henri Pirenne has underlined the great role of "accident" in history. An important battle can often be decided by pure chance. A sudden death may remove a man's worst enemy. The skill or lack of skill that characterizes the head of state or the military leader who at a particular moment happens to have political or military responsibility—this may determine which side will gain the victory. Erroneous reports can lead to mistaken measures. The ballot in a legislative assembly may be so evenly divided in a given case that the outcome has to be decided by the casting of lots.

The question in all such cases is the extent of the consequences that this coincidence may have had. One can ask whether it has merely delayed or hastened a result that would have come about in any case, or whether that which seemed to be a matter of pure chance had a deeper connection.

I have myself studied a few cases of this kind. I believe I have shown that the feeble policy of England in its conduct of the war against the rebellious American colonies had its cause in particular circumstances in English society and politics.[2] Other scholars have shown the same for

English policy on the European continent during the Revolutionary wars in France.[3]

Each individual case requires this kind of careful restudy. But the whole question is also connected with the basic approach of modern historical research.

European historians from the time of Thucydides have always assumed that historical events had their causes. Even those who have maintained that God determined everything have assumed that he ruled wisely and according to a plan, so that there would be a connection between the events. Gradually, however, scholars came to realize that there might be two distinct kinds of causes. The early historians were satisfied when they could uncover the *immediate* causes of events, the motives of the people who were responsible for them. This is still an indispensable part of historical research, but Polybius pointed out two thousand years ago that the organization of society and the state was also an important factor in determining the victory or defeat of a people. The great historical thinkers of the eighteenth century, Montesquieu and those who succeeded him, made it crystal clear that it was just as essential to uncover the causes that lay farther back—those that had their origin in social conditions of various kinds, in cultural life, political organization, economic systems, and many other things. In this way the writing of history was elevated into an effort to throw light on the continuity of life itself and to deepen our understanding of the forces that govern human existence.

This mode of thought inevitably had its effect on the course of historical research. In the first place, the question of coincidence was thrust aside, or at least subordinated in the discussions. Chance could not play too great a part when it was a question of elucidating the general conditions of a whole society. The Belgian scholar Quetelet demonstrated this in 1835 by employing statistics in the analysis of social conditions. Besides this, there also developed a new way of looking at historical sources.

Leopold Ranke was one of the first to point out that historical writings and other reports from early times are often colored by the partisanship of the authors in the social and political struggles of their age, so that one needs to take this into account in judging their reliability. In Scandinavian historianship this point of view was characteristic, for example, of the critique that Curt Weibull made (in 1910) of the medieval Danish historian Saxo Grammaticus. But there was another point of view that penetrated even more deeply into the problem, because it turned its attention to the intellectual connection between the ancient historians and their contemporaries. We know well enough from our own time that those who interpret the past to us are bound by the modes of thought and the interests of the life around them. Should not the same be true of earlier historians? In reality it was quite common to look on the old Greek and Latin historians in this way. This was what made them vital forces in the intellectual life of our times. Yet I met opposition in 1913 when I advocated the application of the same point of view to the Icelandic sagas that dealt with the history of Norway, particularly the greatest of them all, the *Heimskringla*, by Snorri Sturluson.[4] Since that time it has become a commonplace of historical thinking that historians derive from their contemporaries the light in which they see the past.

The renowned German critic Lessing was, I believe, the first to point out that final truths could not be established in history because every new generation had to look at the past with new eyes, ask new questions, and find new answers, just as surely as each generation had to recreate its religious faith even when the words remained unchanged. I recall when the distinguished Belgian historian Henri Pirenne presented his new view on the origin of capitalism in the Middle Ages at the Congress of Historians in London in 1913. In concluding he said, "All theories fall. Mine will also fall. I believe, however, that I have at least taken one step forward in the direction of truth." This is what every new scholar must strive for—to see history as truly as it is possible for him to do.

This applies to the criticism of sources as well as to synthesis, to the individual facts and the connection between them, to the psychology of the individual and of society. The methods of this research have grown more and more refined. We still continue to ask for causes and motivations, and since life is always changing we must always be looking for its basic forces.

History has learned from natural science that it will not do to speculate abstractly on our problems. We must work inductively and build on factual experience.

Chapter III

RELIGION AS A SOCIAL FORCE

Religion is a word with many meanings. There is scarcely another word that has been interpreted in so many different ways. If there is any kind of a common denominator, we might perhaps say that it is a faith in higher powers outside or above ourselves.

If this were nothing more than a conclusion one could arrive at by logical thinking, it could not have become the force in human life that it has. When religion becomes a living faith that helps to give strength to one's will and deed, then it gains a great place for itself.

A faith on this foundation can assume a virtually endless number of forms. In his great epic poem about human history, *Man, Creation, and Messiah* (1830), Henrik Wergeland viewed religion as something highly personal:

> Every human soul
> Has in itself a chapel of its own.
> Easier it would be to find two straws alike
> Than two human beings
> Who worship and believe alike.

Even if this may be true of people living in the most highly cultivated societies of our day, it is probably correct to maintain, as did Karl Lamprecht in his historical writings, that the farther back we go into time, the more we see how strongly people were bound by the conventions and customs of their society. This made it possible for religion to become a social force from the very beginning— indeed, one of the basic forces in social life. Religion came to play an important role in the struggle for human existence and in this way helped to satisfy the very first need of man, his simple craving for nourishment and protection.

Primitive peoples could only conceive that mysterious higher forces directed wind and weather, sun and moon, the growth of the soil, birth and death among man and beast—indeed, everything that stirred in nature. They inevitably personified these powers and classified them into good and evil. The evil ones were those who did harm to man. They became nasty trolls whom it was necessary to fight and overcome. The good powers were those from whom one might expect help and whom it was therefore important to have as friends if things were going to turn out for the best for men and their livelihoods. Such powers could become gods to whom one prayed and made offerings. Believing this, men were bound together. They could unite and gain additional strength to frighten away evil spirits. They could gather in prayer and sacrifice to gods and good spirits. A sacrificial festival forged a bond both among the participants themselves and with the god around whom they gathered. Out of this grew a society.

A new theme entered religion when the belief arose that man had a spirit or soul that continued to live after the body had died. The dead spirits could also be either friendly or hostile. It might become necessary to keep them locked in their graves, or they might demand special sacrifices at the places where they lived in the earth. Burial customs arose that were common to greater or smaller groups. The very faith in life after death might prove to be a new force in human life.

To be sure, religion was nowhere the only force that united men into societies. There were other factors from the very beginning. All men have within themselves the need that psychologists have called "the group instinct." Aristotle already pointed out that man was a *zóon politikón*, a political animal. This instinct is one we even find in animals. It may be asked whether this group instinct in its core may not be identical with the religious impulse—a need to seek protection and help from someone greater and more powerful than oneself. This need can find its satisfaction by turning either to invisible powers or to one's fellow men, or even to one single man, the chief. It is a need that can find its outlet in religion as well as in the construction of a social order.

In societies where religion played an important role, one or more men commonly arose who had special talents and knowledge in all that was called religion or magic. Such a man became the great leader of his people in such questions, and directed their sacrifices or their sorcery. The ethnologists have often used the Mongol word *shaman* for this middleman between the spirits (or gods) and man. In some societies he also became the secular leader. This was not the usual thing, but it testifies to the power of religion in the formation of society.

In all social life firm rules of organization—one might even call them laws—were necessary for human relations, or in other words, society demanded a morality, an ethics. This need not have its root in religion, but as long as supernatural forces or gods were thought to direct virtually everything in life, it was understandable that moral laws should also be regarded as having been dictated by the gods. They became "God's commandments" to man and were thereby given religious consecration. We all know the Ten Commandments, which the Jewish Jahve proclaimed to Moses on Mount Sinai. He was neither the first nor the only giver of moral laws. Everywhere it came to be considered a "sin"—a crime against the divine powers—to do anything that contravened the sacred morality of society.

In this way religion joined forces from the very beginning with other social currents. It is virtually impossible to separate it out from the others and to say when religion alone is the motivating force, and which other forces have contributed to what is called religion. This is true from the very start of the three great religions that today have the greatest dominion in the world—the Christian, the Mohammedan, and the Buddhist.

Buddhism, the oldest of them, might almost be called a religion without a religion. God or gods have no part in it. And Buddha virtually made faith in life after death into a threat. He established it as the purpose of human life that one be saved from living. Man was supposed to exert all his powers to free himself from all worldly bonds and his soul from all kinds of worldly, egotistic desires. If he was unsuccessful, his soul was condemned to come back and live life over, to try once more, or even time after time in that purgatory that was life. Victory came when he could die the perfect death, so that his soul entered into the great universal soul. Some historians have said that this was a philosophy rather than a religion, and that this doctrine lacked the mysticism that is the vital force in all religion. It seems to me, however, that there is more than enough mysticism in the doctrine of transmigration. The main thing, however, is that it became the basis of a powerful ethical system. The five commandments of Buddhism that state the rules for right living are just as negative as most of the Mosaic commandments, with their regulations for everything one is supposed not to do. The positive element behind this negative doctrine is the requirement that one shall not live for oneself but for other people. Loving one's neighbor is the life rule of the true Buddhist. If he lives honorably and well according to this doctine, he will be "saved." In this way religion, or faith, is bound indissolubly together with ethics, a combination that has made it possible for Buddhism to become a cultural force in the Asian world.

Buddha himself had no idea of building a distinct religious society. His successors gradually parted company with others who taught differently from themselves, and they built their own temples and had their own priests. The same was true of Christianity. Jesus of Nazareth did not wish to break with ancient Jewish teaching. On the contrary, he constantly referred his disciples to "the law and the prophets." Their words were to be followed and obeyed. He took from Judaism the two greatest articles of faith in his religion—the belief in an almighty God, and the belief in bliss or punishment in the life hereafter. The strongest basis for his religious teaching came from the heritage he derived from the past. His great complaint against those who taught the traditional religion of his day, the Pharisees, was that they put too much stress on outward customs, on prayers, sacrifices, and fasting. What he, Jesus, wanted was to shift the emphasis to the inner attitude, to the will of man. His demand on men was for a living love of one's neighbor, a love that would embrace all men, even their enemies. It was a demand that went farther and deeper than any that had previously been made in any religion. As he himself said, it would make all believers into brothers. They were brothers also because they were all God's children—God was their father. Even if one grants with Freud that the concept of fatherhood is at the heart of all concepts of divinity, it must be said that the idea gained a new accent in the Christian gospel and so made Christianity in truth a new religion. Even if Christians still were supposed to fear God, they should above all love him. Love of God and one's fellow men was the central message that was to unite all those who followed Jesus. This teaching bore within it a tremendous power that made it possible to build a great society of brothers. This became the Christian church.

We all know that the church that sprang into being after the death of Jesus became something more, and also something less, than He had dreamed. The church gradually evolved a body of religious teachings, a theology, which was extraneous to anything He had taught, and took its starting point in the idea that He was not only God's son, but also God himself. Even if the commandment of love remained in force, it was not allowed to remain at all times the central feature either in teaching or in action. But it always acted as a leaven in Christian society, and made Christianity into a truly cultural and constructive force in social life.

The teachings of Jesus involved not only a religious revolution but to some extent a social revolution as well. He turned particularly to the poor when he traveled around the country, to fishermen and other "little" people. He found his followers among them, and for a long time Christianity remained a religion of the lower classes. Things changed as Christianity gradually won power in society, and the feeling of social brotherhood could then be transmuted in various ways.

The demand of Jesus on the rich man that he part with

his wealth and give all he owned to the poor never became a general law in Christian countries, though it left deep traces in the churches themselves. The monks gave up all personal property, and in the early periods they also withdrew from all worldly society. The demand on the rich was reduced to a tenth of their income or inheritance to assist the poor. All such philanthropic aid acquired a religious motivation by being associated with the idea of the donor's eternal salvation. In one way this could be looked upon as an egotistic idea: the donor was giving for his own sake. Basically, however, this was founded on the idea that God was served by doing good. Religion and ethics here fused in a higher unity. The great church fathers affirmed this doctrine, and the Christian churches began to organize help for the poor, so that this became an activity of the social order.

It is a remarkable thing that Christianity, which had its origin in an Asiatic people, found its strongest response in Europe and became the special religion of the peoples of Europe. To be sure, we have learned in very recent times that in the earliest centuries there was a good deal of Christianity in some parts of central Asia. For the most part, Christianity in that area was destroyed by main force. It is possible, however, that Christianity had greater spiritual affinity with European than with Asiatic culture, except for Judaism, precisely because the western countries of Asia already had been drawn into the cultural life of Europe.

A good half millennium after Jesus a new religious movement arose in western Asia, one that was to find its most enduring foothold in Asia and Africa. This was Mohammedanism. This religion also involved a revolution, which like that of Christianity was at the same time social, ethical, and religious. Mohammed was indignant about the rapacious commercial rulers of his home city, Mecca, and the godless life of its wealthy classes. His religious needs were not satisfied by all the local and minor deities whom the Arabs worshiped. He sought strength in the almighty God whom he had learned to know from Christian and especially from Jewish teaching, and he had an inner conviction that he himself was called to be a prophet and a crusader for this true god, Allah. With support from the farm population around the little town that later won the name Medina-en-nabi, or the City of the Prophet, he declared war on Mecca. Then he proceeded to organize not only a religious society but also a state that would carry his religion, Islam, out into the world. The demand this religion made on its followers was faith in and obedience to Allah, a just god who would reward all those who followed his commandments with eternal bliss and punish all the unrepentant sinners. He also demanded obedience to the prophet and the laws he had collected in the Koran. The substance of this book was justice among men and war against all who would not bow their knees to Allah. This religion differed rather notably from the emphasis on love in Christianity and Buddhism. But here too the ethical demands were sanctified and strengthened by religious faith.

The point I have been attempting to clarify is this: that when men worked their way up from their belief in all kinds of spirits and creatures, religion acquired an ethical content for them, and God became a guardian and a judge of their morality. The transition to this new life could take place in various ways, and it was always a complex and intricate development. Religious faith was never the only motivation.

As these new religious societies grew in strength, the interplay between various psychological forces could become even more manifold, and it could grow still more difficult to distinguish the extent to which religion played a part in the course of events. I shall not try to show this by surveying the entire history of religion or the churches, but I do think it may be useful to study some cases or problems in which religion has played more or less of a part and try to find out the actual connection so far as possible. I limit myself to Christianity and to my personal researches in Christian history.

First I wish to consider the problem of the connection between Christianity and the liberation of slaves in the Middle Ages. It has often been said and generally believed that Christians must of necessity regard slavery as something unnatural and contrary to religion because the Christian teachings brought with them a new respect for the individual human being, all of whom were equal before God. As a consequence it is supposed that in all Christian countries slavery had to disappear. From the point of view of Norwegian history this idea is particularly tempting, since we find in the oldest Christian laws of Norway a decree that every year one man shall be liberated in each district. This does not amount to a great deal, but does suggest that in the eleventh and twelfth centuries giving slaves their freedom was regarded as a good Christian deed. But if we turn to other countries, which were Christianized long before Norway, the sources tell an entirely different story.

I have pored over hundreds of decisions and decrees issuing from all kinds of ecclesiastical councils, local as well as universal, and from popes and bishops of the Middle Ages, without finding a single injunction or admonition to liberate slaves.[5] I have found a formula for the liberation of slaves from a somewhat uncertain time, possibly Frankish or Visigothic of the eighth century, which says that one should liberate one's slave "for the salvation of one's soul and for eternal reward." Such liberation is held to be similar to other privileges that one gives up or debt that one forgives. The liberation takes place in a church. It was a demand of the church that this should always be done, and the church maintained that all who were liberated came under her protection and were therefore particularly bound to the church. Otherwise there is no evidence that the church did anything for liberation.

We do hear from the oldest church councils, those that were held before Christianity became a state religion in the Roman Empire, that admonitions were issued to Christian slaves to be obedient and faithful to their masters, even if the latter were pagans. Such admonitions were no longer necessary after the state had made Christianity the sole religion of the Empire. The church continued to protect each man's right to keep slaves by requiring, for example, its own servants to return any slaves that had escaped from their owners. Indeed, the church itself came to own slaves as it gradually acquired landed property. The church could receive slaves as gifts and could even buy them. Then regulations were established concerning possible liberation of such ecclesiastical slaves. In these regulations it was stated that no cleric lower than a bishop had the right to free them, and even the bishop was limited to certain procedures established in the laws.

There was only one single area in which the church was opposed to slavery. This was when landed property had fallen into the hands of Jews. Christians were not allowed to work for Jews, the old enemies of Christ. In practice this idea led to a demand that Jews should not be allowed to own land, and in this way the Jews were driven into commerce and handicrafts. The Christian slaves were not the ones who stood to benefit from this rule.

Instead, the church urged all its people to be kind to their slaves, to take good care of them, to let them have Sundays off, and not punish them with unreasonable severity. As time went on, the church itself established punishments for those who treated their slaves too badly, who killed them, or maimed them, or punished them with as many as a hundred lashes. This was particularly enforced for the slaves owned by the church itself. Regulations were adopted stating that the work loads of slaves on church property should be less than those on private property. Pope Gregory the Great was the one who established this regulation around the year 600. It did not become standard practice, however, until the ninth century when even the length of the working day was established for the church slaves. Slaves were gradually being regarded more and more as human beings with the usual social privileges. They could own property. They could appear as witnesses in court, etc.

This was due to the fact that the slaves had come to be bound to the soil, or the farm, not to the personal owner. The church had its share in this development, since it never parted with land it had acquired, and therefore the slaves who lived on church property never changed owners. The same was true of other landed estates inherited through several generations of one family. We see that the very word for slave—*servus*—changed its meaning so that it came to be synonymous with "the one who is bound to the land," the serf. This social transformation resulted in the disappearance from society of the old caste of slaves. For this reason it was possible for a church council in London in 1102 to forbid the ugly old custom of selling people as if they were animals. A Hungarian bishop's council in 1114 decreed a ban forbidding any bishop or priest to have slaves in their congregations. A church council in Toulouse in 1119 forbade anyone from making a free man or woman into a slave. It is against this background that we must see the Norwegian regulation in the old Christian law. It was no longer regarded as right to keep people in slavery.

Christianity had of course assisted in this development, but only because it demanded a more humanitarian treatment of the slaves. No religious principle was established in this way. We know that when Negro slavery arose in modern times, it took a long time before the Christian church opposed it. The universal ideas on human rights of the eighteenth century did at least as much to stir the consciences of people to see the evils of the new slavery. We can see the union of secular-humanistic and Christian ideas in the discussion of this question among the Unitarians of New England. The struggle against Negro slavery both in England and in America was initiated by such dissenting Christian sects as the Quakers and Methodists. In America, however, the Methodist church was split on the question, and the more official churches remained outside, or even took up a position which opposed the freedom of the slaves. There was not always a spirit of social revolt in Christianity!

Yet it did come to pass that a Christian revolution turned against the Christian church itself. This is what happened in the great heretical movements of western Europe from the eleventh century on.

These heretical movements were of an entirely different kind from the ones that are called heresy in the orthodox histories of the early church. At that time the struggle concerned the question of which doctrine should be regarded as the true faith, and those who lost were condemned as heretics. When we reach the latter half of the Middle Ages, the problems that cause controversy are not primarily theological in nature. It is true that their opponents called the revolutionaries "heretics," applying to them such words as "Manichaeans." I doubt, however, that there was anyone at that time who had a very clear notion of what Manichaeanism was. Most of them had only read in Augustine that in his time he had struggled against Manichaeans in Africa, and so this became a suitable term of abuse to apply to the rebels. This damned them immediately, just as when orthodox people in our day have cried "freethinker."

The heretical movements of the late Middle Ages arose in the lowest strata of society. We first hear about them from Milan in the middle of the eleventh century. In the twelfth century they appear in other cities of northern Italy, in Lyon and other cities of southern France, in German cities of the Rhine region, and in the Netherlands. From Milan it is said that "because of their poverty" they were called *patarines*, and this word was translated as "linen weavers." We hear from France also that they were called "weavers." This tells us what kind of people the leaders in this movement must have been. They were working people, unlearned people, who did not understand the Latin church language and who for the most part could not even read. It is clear that when such people were called up for hearings and cross-examined on what they believed about this or that point in the doctrine of the church, they could easily stray into heretical opinions. They might happen to say that they thought it was wrong to baptize children, since children understood nothing of the baptismal ritual. They might say that they did not understand the eucharistic doctrine about the transformation of bread into flesh, or, worse yet, they could not believe in the sacrament of communion, since the ministers were not worthy to administer it.

Here we come to a central feature in their heresy: they

complained that the ministers took money for their work and lived in drunkenness and riotous living, not in the poverty and temperance that was fitting for the servants of Christ according to the gospel. They had acquired the simple gospel of Jesus, and they wanted this to be the law of life in the church for all Christians. To this end they did not need priests. It was enough if they followed the teaching of the gospel. They called themselves for the most part *katharoi*, that is, "pure" (I do not know where they picked up this elegant Greek word; on German soil it became the word *ketter*, that is, "heretic"). Their intention was to live a life free of all worldly desire. Wealth was sin, or at least a temptation to sin, and rich people were the enemies of a truly Christian society.

We see here a social revolt. The new industrial workers, a class of workmen created by the young textile industry, rose against the landlords and their clerical servants. For this reason many historians have called these heretical movements a social uprising, a revolt of the lower classes. Others have preferred to maintain the view of that period that the heretics revolted against the church and the true faith, so that the religious element was the main feature of the revolt.

The question was taken up as a major topic at the International Congress of Historians in Rome in 1955, where comprehensive discussions were presented orally and in writing. I too ventured to take the floor, because of my extensive work with the social and religious history of the Middle Ages. I believed it was possible to unite these points of view by adopting a psychological approach. I emphasized that these heretics did not revolt against the doctrines which were taught by the church, but against the unevangelic way in which the church was ruled and the even less evangelic way in which the priests of the church lived. The basis of their revolt was moral indignation. It was quite natural that this indignation should find a religious expression, for they were eager to revive true Christianity. But in preaching the ideal of poverty, the demand that no one should yearn for wealth or accumulate the goods of this world, they entered into a social conflict which was born of new social conditions. In this way religious, ethical, and social demands were intertwined in their intellectual and emotional life and became a unity it is not possible to disentangle.

One after the other all of these heretical movements were struck down by fire and sword—the Albigensians in France in the thirteenth century, the Lollards in England in the fourteenth century, and the Hussites in Bohemia in the fifteenth century. In all of them we find fused the three motives I have mentioned. This was the reason that ecclesiastical and secular authorities united to crush them.

Since that time many movements have arisen that in their origin greatly resembled the heretical movements of the Middle Ages. We may mention the Hauge movement in Norway. This was also suppressed to begin with, though it later won the approval of the church for the very reason that it did not raise a standard of revolt against orthodox doctrine. Therefore historians have traditionally ignored the feature in the movement that in reality was squarely contrary to orthodox Lutheranism, namely, its emphasis on good deeds (rather than on the true faith). It just happens that historically this was the oldest form of Christianity.

The heretical revolts of the Middle Ages did not succeed in splitting the church until they also turned against its basic doctrines. The result was the creation of all the new church bodies, both Lutheran and Reformed. Again, other historical causes were also involved, and it is well worth our trouble to look somewhat more carefully at this event.

When the heretics took up cudgels against the priesthood of the church, they were also refusing obedience to the highest official of that church, the pope. Throughout the Middle Ages, but most vigorously in its last two centuries, another power had grown up that also wanted to throw off its allegiance to the pope. This was the government of the national states. The outward expression of the victory of heresy was the rejection by a government of the power of the pope. And Luther proclaimed that the pope was his enemy forever.

Even before this time, demands for national independence had arisen within the church. Such demands were strengthened at this very time, the beginning of the fourteenth century, by the schism in the papacy, which brought into being two or even three competing popes. A vigorous ruler, like Queen Margaret in Scandinavia, could seize the opportunity to gain power over the bishops of her own country. In France a royal decree of 1408 affirmed that the pope had no control over the French church—or the "Gallic" church, as it was then called. The king founded his argument on theoretical elucidations by the professors at the Sorbonne, who had imported the theory from England. There it had been taught in connection with the heretical movement of the Lollards. One ruler after the other began to make formal treaties, or concordats, with the pope about the rule of the church. The fact that countries like France, Spain, and Portugal remained Catholic and were not drawn into the Reformation is to a great extent due, I believe, to the fact that they had attained ecclesiastical independence without a rejection of the church doctrines.[6]

It was mostly in the German-speaking countries, from Switzerland to the Netherlands, that the Reformation was borne by a folk movement. Here it was primarily the ecclesiastical abuses, especially the trade in indulgences, that called forth the reformers to do battle. We should not overlook the fact that Luther and other leaders were driven to revolt by a problem of conscience. Behind the heretical doctrines they enunciated there was a deep religious need that could not be satisfied with indulgences, or the forgiveness of sins from priest or pope, and that could not tolerate having a saint as middleman. They had to go straight to God himself with their remorse. If, however, they were going to overcome the resistance of the old church, they had to ask help and protection from the rulers of the land. These were often impelled by other motives, which were at least as powerful. Luther himself appealed to the concept of German nationalism as early as 1520 in his exhortation, "To the Christian Nobility of German Nationality." In this he described how the pope and his foreign servants were sucking Germany dry and had made its people into their slaves. In Switzerland Zwingli was also as much a national as a religious figure. Many north German princes made use of the Reformation to free themselves of both emperor and pope. Others, like the duke of Bavaria and the archduke of Austria, secured profitable agreements, especially economic ones, with the pope, and therefore remained Catholics. In 1525, when the Grand Master of the German Order, after consultation with Luther, made Prussia into a hereditary dukedom, the political motive was at least as strong as the religious one.

Outside of Germany political motives could play an even more prominent part and might be wholly decisive. The English King Henry VIII did indeed play theologian and prepare learned defenses of the Lutheran doctrine, but he proclaimed himself the leading churchman of the country in 1530 on an entirely secular basis. On the strength of this he acquired for himself both the property and the income of the church. Gustavus Vasa of Sweden had done exactly the same thing three years earlier. Gustavus's argument to the parliament of Västerås that year was based on the financial distress of the state. The annual expenses were two and one-half times as great as the income, and there were debts both abroad and at home. The remedy he recommended was to take over the property of the church and the monasteries. When the ecclesiastical estate, that is, the bishops, said that they were bound by their oath to the pope never to part with any of their property, and when the noble estate supported them, the king pounded his fist on the table and wept. He told them he would no longer be king if this was the way he was going to be treated. Through this ultimatum he succeeded in getting his will, and the consequence was that now the king became the supreme ruler of the church in Sweden instead of the pope, and the Swedish church became a state church. The only enactment that concerned religion proper was an injunction to preach the gospel in pure and undiluted form through-out the kingdom, and it was left to the king to provide for this. Lutheran doctrine did gradually come into force in the Swedish churches, but it was twenty years before it was officially established. The initiation of the Reformation in Sweden was a purely political decision.

The events in Denmark were not quite as one-sided. Here, at least, there had been Lutheran preaching for some ten to fifteen years. But the nobles from Holstein that helped Christian III to the throne had certainly been strengthened in their Lutheranism by the prospect of laying hands on the property of the church. The immediate background of the coup of 1536 in Copenhagen was a demand for pay by the army. Under the king and the council of nobles a purely "secular rule" was introduced. The church was subjected to the government of the state, which would take care that the pure word of God was properly preached throughout the kingdom. Pastors friendly to the Reformation helped to set up the new ecclesiastical system, so there were at least some religious elements in the new order.

This was not true at all in Norway. Just as the kingdom of Norway was made subject to Denmark by force of arms in 1537, so the Danish church ordinance of the same year was introduced into Norway by decision of the Danish royal council. In this country there had been no popular participation in the religious movement. There were practically no other Lutherans in the country than the German merchants in Bergen. The Reformation here was nothing but a royal proclamation. The same was true in Iceland. It should be emphasized that these were extreme cases. Otherwise the Reformation was not purely a matter of force. But almost everywhere religion *was* exploited for political purposes. Religious movements were not allowed to spread freely, but were made subservient to powers and forces of quite a different kind.

In the wake of the Reformation came an age of religious wars. Here it did indeed prove possible to arouse a genuine religious frenzy on both sides. The two enemy camps, the Catholic and the Reformed churches, condemned one another with all possible vigor. They were heartily convinced that all who had a different faith from themselves would surely go to hell. In this struggle faith was certainly preferred to good deeds, a faith anchored to dogmatic structures that in themselves had little to do with Jesus' basic commandment of love. One may therefore ask, with some justice, whether these conflicts should be called *religious* wars. It was hardly the fundamental tenets of Christianity that started them on their course.

On the Catholic side, the leader himself, Emperor Charles V, who had a difficult time keeping his empire united, tried for a time to eliminate religion from the war. He wanted only, he said, to make war against rebels who refused to obey the law and who disregarded decisions of the Reichstag and the judgments of the courts. He did, however, want to make Germany Catholic, and even if he was willing to relax some of the Catholic doctrines, the Protestants were unrelenting. In a temporary armistice for Germany agreement was reached on the principle of *cujus regio, illius religio*, that is, that the ruler of each country should decide its religion. This meant that the decisive factor should be the purely political regime, not what people in each country thought or believed. No one was willing to show tolerance for deviations in faith.

This could not remain anything more than an armistice, which was finally broken by the Thirty Years' War. Once more religion and politics were infiltrated in one another. Even in a deeply religious man like Gustavus Adolphus of Sweden historical research has uncovered political motivations involving the rivalry between Sweden and Poland. One need hardly mention that the Catholic country of France, under the rule of a papal cardinal, assisted the Protestants of Germany. In this way the religious war turned into a struggle for political power. In the sphere of international politics religion and morality have regularly had to yield to other considerations—the thought of power and economic advantage.

The historical events I have here sketched are sufficient to show the role of religion in politics. Religion has been so confused with purposes of other kinds that it has been transformed into something that may seem to be the exact opposite of its own fundamental teaching. Yet this too follows from the nature of the basic religious urge. An active religious faith quite naturally fosters the conviction that this faith is the only thing that can save mankind. This may lead to missionary activity, but it may also breed fanaticism.

The psychological trait that made people see enemies in those who embraced other forms of religion, even within one and the same Christian community, not only roused one nation against another, but also drove wedges into individual nations and led to civil war. Here too, other motivations could supplement the religious one. We see this most clearly in England in the religio-democratic uprising that found its leader in Cromwell. We meet here two opposed types of people, both socially and religiously different. On the one hand stood the gay and lighthearted nobleman who found it natural to follow the king and the church, while on the other hand stood the solid and serious citizen who took God with him in his daily life—cavalier vs. puritan. In this contrast we see how the dogmatic difference could actually be an expression of contrary temperaments and contrary views of life.

Max Weber[7] maintained that English Puritanism, and other movements of the same kind, such as Pietism and Methodism, led to a new spirit in economic life, which he called the "spirit of capitalism." He pointed out how the Puritans were led to regard themselves as God's chosen people. They turned their lives into a striving for the honor of God and had to show in their deeds that their faith was a living force. They could not waste anything that might serve this purpose, and it was a duty for them to multiply the "talents" God had entrusted to them. Weber portrayed their economic ethic in such a way that many thought he believed this to be the origin of modern capitalism. This was not what he really meant to say. He only wished to demonstrate one of the intellectual presuppositions of capitalism. To some extent he was quite right: we can observe the connection both in England and in America. But the spirit of capitalism itself had roots that were not just the obligation to save money and to make good use of capital that had been scraped together. It also had its roots in a need and a will to organize a whole community of workers for large economic purposes, which is a motivation of a quite different kind. This was the middle-class or bourgeois society seeking power and wealth. Puritanism was a force in economic life only to the extent that it helped to shape the bourgeois spirit.

Religion played a much more active role in the internal politics of these countries and in their government. This did not always mean, as often during the religious wars, that religion became a servant of politics. The original purpose was rather that religion should govern politics. History can tell us that this idea did occasionally prevail.

As far as I know Charlemagne was the first ruler who clearly and systematically established Christianity as the foundation of a government. This was especially true after he became emperor and felt it as his calling to be the trustee of all Christendom. He sent specially appointed officials around to find out how the people were being ruled in his empire. In his instructions to these emissaries he wrote:

Wherever it appears that anything in the laws causes inequity or injustice, they shall investigate this closely and take note of it so that the Emperor with the help of God can remedy it. No one must be emboldened to transgress the law by aggression or duplicity, as many are wont to do, or to harm the churches of God, or the poor, or widows and orphans, or any Christian man. All shall live in justice according to the commandment of God, and every man shall be faithful in his service or his occupation.

The servants of the church shall live according to the Canon Law without grasping commercial activities. Nuns shall obey the laws of their cloister. Laymen and seculars shall keep the law without fail, and all shall live with each other in perfect love and peace. The emissaries themselves shall listen carefully if anyone complains over injustice he has suffered. In so far as they wish to have the grace of the Almighty God and keep their promises, they shall everywhere fulfill the law and the demands of justice in obedience to the will of God, whether it be a question of the holy churches of God, or the poor, the widows and orphans, or the people as a whole.

This, then, is a program of government based on an official Christian morality. It speaks of law and justice, but at the same time it breathes the spirit of Christian love. Though using words taken from the Mosaic law, it emphasizes the protection to be given to the poor, to widows, and to orphans. This is the blueprint of a Christian welfare state. For Emperor Charlemagne it was not just an empty gesture. He organized laws and courts, and he hindered the use of force and vengeance as far as he was able. In the instructions to his emissaries he also wrote:

We vigorously condemn the killings which destroy so many Christian persons. If the Lord has forbidden those who believe in him to nourish hate and enmity, how much more does he not oppose their committing murder! Because we do not wish that the people that have been entrusted to us shall be wiped out for this sin, we condemn it severely. And because we do not wish that sin shall grow so that enmity arises among Christians, therefore we command that if the devil causes the killing of men, the guilty one shall immediately repent and give payment to the kinsmen of the victim. We absolutely forbid the relations of the dead one to aggravate the sin with new enmity, or to refuse to give the killer peace when he has paid his fine.

In a historical study I wrote in 1903, I said about Charlemagne: "Even if his institutions did not in the end survive, he established an ideal of law in the hearts of peoples and governments, and he made everyone conscious of the fact that the state should be the champion of justice."[8] We find it again in his successors, and this brought with it an intimate cooperation between state and church—a cooperation that historians, particularly Protestant historians, often have forgotten because they have considered only the conflict that later arose between state and church. Beginning particularly with the time of Charlemagne, state and church worked together to promote Christian enlightenment and gentler customs. There were many occasions and long periods when this cooperation might fail or disappear, but the ideal was established and never died. The state, which had been built on force, became a state built on law.

If we go back to the oldest history of Norway, we can probably say that a state built on law had been established in Norway even before Christianity came to this country. Even though the first Norwegian laws were not written down until after Christianity, it is clear that they have their roots deep in the past, and that the basic principles of justice are older than Christianity.[9] Christian thinking soon began to affect the development of law, however, particularly in the great legal revision completed in the reign of King Magnus the Law-mender (1263–1280). At this time the judges were exhorted in the law code itself not to judge severely, according to the letter of the old laws, but to consider all mitigating circumstances in the crimes and to remember that Justice had a sister whose name was Mercy. Mercy (or Grace) was a new word and a new idea, created by Christianity. It was adopted into the very title of the king, "By the Grace of God," and it became a special activity of the king to give mercy. It was at this time that Norwegian kings began to build prisons, in which they kept thieves and other criminals in confinement instead of having them executed or maimed. It is quite possible that the thieves themselves were not especially happy about being put in prison, "the dark room," but the prisons were at least a testimonial to the fact that the authorities no longer enjoyed killing people, preferring instead to turn them over to the mercy of God.

Christianity is not the only factor in this development. A great deal in Christianity was an inheritance from ancient Roman law. Both law and morality gradually acquired a life of their own and influenced the activities of state and society without any direct connection with Christianity. But Christianity had powerfully assisted in the shaping of that morality, which gained more and more foothold among men. We can often be in doubt as to whether the backgrounds of social events are to be found in Christian or in secular morality.

The eighteenth century was the period of enlightenment, with a great breakthrough in the care of all the weaker members of society—children and old people, the blind, the maimed, and the ill. Before this time the church had provided much of this. Now the secular authorities undertook an even more universal social care. It was a period of disbelief in religious dogmas and of falling away from Christianity, but the desire to help and to take part in deeds of love was at least as much alive among non-Christians as among Christians. This was because a universal social morality had grown up that was now a law for everyone.

Nor must we forget that even the unbelievers and the non-Christians had their religion, though a kind different from the Christian one. This was a faith in human progress and a will to mutual human helpfulness without thought of God or eternal life. It was a faith that imposed upon everyone certain moral and social responsibilities, and thereby stimulated a universal human brotherhood without limitations of class or nation. This too was a religion, because it made people sense that there were forces greater than themselves. It was a religion that has left its mark on state and society in our own times. Its history is therefore not as old as Christianity's, but it is still a historical force of great importance.

Chapter IV

THE SPIRIT OF COOPERATION IN STATE AND NATION

When Darwin in 1859 launched his doctrine of the "struggle for existence" as the greatest basic force in nature, he did the converse of what historians and sociologists have often done. He applied to nature the laws of human life that he believed he had observed in the competitive and power-hungry society in which he lived. Malthus had outlined the nature of this society twenty years earlier with devastating consistency.[10] In his next major work, *The Descent of Man* (1871), Darwin made important reservations in his law of survival when he pointed out the importance that "social virtues" had in the struggle for existence, both of animals and of men. Twenty years later the anarchist Kropotkin pointed out the tremendous importance in human progress of the spirit of cooperation that one could observe in all fields of natural and human society. One could go so far as to say that society is the thing that has preserved the human race down through the ages.

Many have expressed it as their opinion that the chief trait of "wild" peoples, barbarians, that distinguishes them from civilized peoples is their pugnacity—what psychologists call "the instinct of aggression" and have considered as one of the natural instincts of man. Now of course we do not know very much about the nature of life among the earliest human beings—this is mostly guesswork. It may be worth noting, however, that archeologists have not found any weapons of combat from the oldest periods. For the most part they have found only tools for peaceful activities. Whatever weapons there are were clearly intended for hunting, or they are hooks that were used to catch fish in the sea. It is most interesting to observe that one of the earliest evidences of social life on Norwegian soil is the stone quarry at Hespriholmen outside of Bømlo, where people of the Stone Age from all of western Norway cooperated in the quarrying of stone. I was genuinely pleased to see that archaeologist Gutorm Gjessing in his recent work, *Man and Culture* (1953), maintained strongly that primitive man was not aggressive, but preferred to live in peace.

The first permanent cooperative group must presumably have been those women and children whom a man could gather around him. In expanding, this circle must first have included people who lived near to one another, within a distinct section of the country. These people would have a natural need for cooperation in all activities of life. We can only imagine the nature of the organization that they developed. We can get some intimations from fragments of old customs that we find among many peoples in historical times, particularly from those peoples whom we call "primitive" and who still live on a low level of culture. We must not forget, however, that even such peoples have a long history behind them, and that many things may have changed through the ages.

In my youth ethnologists were arguing the question of whether the earliest societies had been constructed on what they called "mother-right" (in German, *Mutterrecht*) or "father-right" (*Vaterrecht*), or in other words, whether kinship, inheritance, and cooperation were based on the mother's or father's side of the family. A doctrine was launched and developed in the 1860's and 1870's which held that "mother-right," or matriarchy, was the original organization among all peoples and only later yielded to a patriarchy. Matriarchal societies were found in active existence among Indians in America and Aborigines in Australia. It was assumed that this kind of society had to be the oldest and had once prevailed everywhere, simply because it differed most from those social forms we knew from civilized peoples and historical times. Scholars then attempted to find the basis of the matriarchy. They invented many different explanations, biological and psychological, economic and social. Some scholars rejected the whole idea, but in the 1890's the matriarchal hypothesis was dominant.

When I studied in Leipzig in the winter of 1897–1898, one of my professors assigned me a paper on the problems of "mother-right" among the ancient Germanic peoples. I worked my way through most of what had been written on the subject in the preceding thirty years, and I studied particularly all the sources that were supposed to support the theory that Germanic society had once been matriarchal. My conclusion was that matriarchy had not been the original form of society throughout the world, and certainly not among the Germanic peoples. I believe that the reasoning in my old article is sound and still valid.[11] I could not accept the idea that social development had been identical in all parts of the world, which could only be supported by twisting historical reports from people with patriarchal societies to prove the existence of an earlier matriarchy. I found it amusing to observe that the old sagas, for example, from Iceland, no sooner mentioned mother's brothers or sister's sons than these passages were taken as evidence that people reckoned their kin on the mother's side—as if we cannot all have mother's brothers and sister's sons!

Fifteen years later, in 1913, a brilliant paper was published by Sigmund Freud, "Totem and Taboo," which gave what I think is the best psychological explanation of how a matriarchal society could come into being. This did not in any way prove that such a society had existed among other peoples than those we already knew had had it. I believe Freud was right in thinking that the totemic religions had their roots in a worship of the father, in which they symbolized the father in a particular animal. All the men in such a totem group considered themselves as brothers, so that they were compelled by their religion to find themselves a bride outside this kinship. I cannot see, however, why such an organization necessarily had to lead to a matriarchy. I cannot believe that the system necessarily had to involve a ceremony of bride-stealing, or that one therefore could conclude from stories of bride-stealings that there must once have been a matriarchy. In fact, I am now inclined to think that marriages were mostly arranged peaceably through bridal purchase. I also believe that the authority of the father regularly was the strongest and kept the sons under control. In most of the nations of Europe a patriarchal society was established in the earliest times, and we know of nothing older among these peoples.

This whole controversy now seems to have vanished. As far as I can see, ethnologists now generally assume that both matriarchy and patriarchy have distinct roots in the earliest times that we can reach, and that each of them has grown up independently of the other.

It is clear in any case that even in the most primitive societies there were conceptions of justice, as well as rules and customs everyone within the group had to obey. Morality and law are among the very oldest products of social life, and the firm backbone of all social history.

It is not a part of my plan to discuss here the growth of law, but I would like to point out that the systems of "father-right" and "mother-right" exemplify a particularly strong social bond that joined men together from the earliest times, namely their kinship. Kinship converted a group of people into what is usually called a *clan*, a word from Scottish Gaelic. In Scotland this social system has maintained itself down to our own time, so that all the members of one clan bear the same family name and have a color as their common symbol.

The bond of kinship was capable of extending its force even beyond the clan and could maintain itself as a living force far down through history. We are familiar with the family feuds of the Icelandic sagas, and the vendettas of Sicily or Corsica. It is well known that kinship has an established position in all codes of law, both ancient and modern.

It is not necessary to say more about this, except to remind the reader of how the bonds of kinship can be used to explain important events in history. I once tried to show that marriages between the great clans in various parts of Norway created the conditions that made possible the union of Norway (about 880) under Harald the Fairhaired.[12] I also expressed the opinion that the early conflicts over the royal power in Norway to a great extent were a struggle between the family of Harald and the family of the earls at Lade.[13] I have applied this point of view also to the connection between Norwegian, Danish, and Swedish noble families at the end of the Middle Ages, which led to Norway's remaining in the union with Denmark. It also led to the absorption of the lower nobility of Norway into the families of the wealthier yeomen and government officials. These examples illustrate how deeply pride of kin can affect the general history of a nation.

Many new factors were added that knit further bonds between men. I have already considered religion as such a social force, one that could bring people together in many ways. In the early days of Christianity, when the Christians were only a minority struggling for its existence, they joined into congregations that usually lived together. I noticed a curious little expression of this once when I was traveling around to view the ruins of the ancient Roman cities of North Africa. I was astonished there to find clear evidences that the Christians had been gathered in separate sections of the city outside the walls, in a kind of ghetto by themselves. Just so, the Jews later dwelt—or were forced to dwell—in their ghettos, separated from the Christians. The word "ghetto" comes from Italy, which is ancient Roman territory.

The sense of unity that could be fostered by such a living together did not of course extend beyond the strictly local community. Only small societies could arise in this way. The resulting economic cooperation was also highly limited in the early period. With respect to agriculture it might extend to whole villages, or in the case of trade, to the larger cities.

If more distant peoples were to be drawn together into any kind of fellowship, other conditions had to be realized. One of the oldest of these was the opportunity for trade and the exchange of goods. Archaeologists have demonstrated that goods could be imported over remarkable distances, and they have discovered the foreign models of much local handicraft.

Many of these small communities eventually expanded into states, thus becoming larger communities with wider borders. We know very little about the origin of such states, though we have a variety of legends about it. These legends have generally been made up much later, as, for example, were those we have from the small Greek states or from Rome. I once made an attempt, through archaeological and onomastic research, to find out when and how the first little states of Norway, the so-called *fylke*, were created.[14] I scrutinized the Norwegian district names enumerated in the Ostrogothic author Jordanes (about 500 A.D.), particularly the three names that correspond to our Ranrike, Romerike, and Ringerike. The word *rike* in these names corresponds most closely to what we now would call *velde*, that is, countries subjugated by force. One may compare the Gothic royal names ending in *-rik*, meaning, "powerful." The same Jordanes also mentions a king from western Norway whose name was Rodulf. It is not clear exactly how large a domain he controlled, but at the very least it must have been on the order of a *fylke*. Now we find that just at this time there was a great deal of warfare in Norway. The centuries between 400 and 600 A.D. constitute the period when most of the *bygdeborger*, or local fortifications, were being built around the country. Whether these were intended for defense or offense, they testify clearly enough to a state of war. This was also the period when native forging of iron and the importation of iron from abroad made notable advances. Iron came to be used more than before for making weapons. This was the time when the sword began to play a major role in warfare. In the grave mounds of the chieftains many more weapons are to be found than earlier. It was my suggestion that this was probably the time when little kingdoms were first established in Norway. If so, it means that the first small states in Norway had their origin in conquest by force of arms, and that they were ruled by military chieftains, or overlords.

This corresponds exactly to what we see in the very oldest states we know, the Assyrian and the Egyptian. Each of these had an autocratic ruler, a military leader, and it seems reasonable to suppose that they were founded on force. The unity of the state was primarily a unity in war, directed against neighboring peoples.

It is worth noting that the word "folk," or people, which we now use about the whole nation, originally meant "army." A military organization was the basis of the first state, and the king was also its general. On this foundation the state eventually grew to become the strongest force for unity in man's social life.

We must not make the mistake, however, of thinking that force alone called the state into being. In many places communication and commerce created mutual interests that could knit people together in wider and wider circles. They might often seek protection for their interests in peaceful organization by law, and not just by force of arms. I believe that we have evidence of this, too, in the early history of Norway. The later sagas, often quite legendary in their nature, found it natural to attribute the creation of such extensive legal areas as the Gulathing and the Frostathing to King Haakon, the foster son of Athelstane, and the Eidsivathing to King Halvdan the Black. It now seems much more probable that all this organizing of a *thing* (a legal area with a common assembly) out of three or more *fylke* is older than the kings. We are here on uncertain historical ground, but it seems most reasonable to suppose that these districts united quite voluntarily and without any kind of force, in order to settle quarrels and problems of conflict among the inhabitants at legally organized assemblies. Later, when the kings had subjugated the whole country, they could draw even wider areas into the old law districts, so that more *fylke* could belong to the large district assemblies. Here the power of the state, in the person of the king, completed the work begun by the local people. In this way the state, with the king as its instrument, became a major force in social organization.

It is comparatively easy to follow this development in the new kingdoms that arose in the Middle Ages. The king was responsible for keeping the peace within his borders. To maintain his position he had to ask for the support of his subjects, beginning with the physical sustenance of himself and his men. This was what was called *veitsle* in Norway, *stud* in Denmark, *skot* in Sweden, and *albergaria* in England. Military organization caused these demands to grow and eventually led to the system we call *feudalism*.

There is hardly any system of political organization that has been more widely discussed or more vehemently debated than feudalism. Its main features should now be clear. Feudalism was a natural consequence of military needs and economic conditions in a state that was relatively primitive and a society that still lived for the most part in a natural economy. We find here an interplay of at least two basic forces in social life. In 1903 I tried to clarify the development of feudalism in the new Germanic kingdoms on the continent from this point of view.[15] I believe the most important of the points I then made are still valid.

I have later tried to show that in Norway the first steps on the road to feudalism were taken near the end of the twelfth century under King Sverre.[16] The same thing happened at about the same time in the other Scandinavian countries, chiefly on the English model. The technical term *sysle*, used in Denmark and Norway, corresponds exactly to the old English *shire* (which referred to the office of ruler). I have also shown that in Scandinavia feudalism was more or less fully established by the end of the thirteenth century.[17]

The chief distinctive feature of feudalism was the fact that the king gave up a part of his power to feudal lords, who were obligated, each in his fief, to provide the king with military assistance, and in return got their reward from the fief that they administered. This system grew up quite naturally in the new states that succeeded the disintegration of the Roman Empire. It was a form of organized cooperation between the ruler of the kingdom and the landed aristocracy. This cooperation appeared to give the lower classes their best security. Therefore it could even happen that free farmers voluntarily submitted themselves and their property to the great landed lords.

Systems of this kind could arise wherever conditions were the same as they were in western Europe in the Middle Ages. In point of fact, even if the legal forms were different, the Roman Empire was ruled in much the same way after it had subjugated all the countries around the Mediterranean. Pro-consuls and pro-prætors, were, on a greater scale, what the vassals came to be in the feudal states: they lived on their provinces and levied their armies there. The same principle goes back to even earlier empires, like the Persian. Curiously enough, we find the Persian word *satrap* applied to some European noblemen in the Middle Ages. Even greater is the similarity to the old Chinese kingdom, where the principle of feudalism bobbed up time after time. In later centuries pure feudalism was established in such countries as Turkey and Japan.

Just as historians have tended to overemphasize the opposition of church and king in the Middle Ages, so they have also overemphasized the struggle between king and nobles. In doing so they have unconsciously projected back into an earlier period the struggle that is so well known in later centuries. As I wrote in 1931:

There was in the beginning no such opposition. On the contrary, it was the king himself who established feudalism. As he gradually changed from a purely military figure to an administrator, the requirements of power compelled him to build up a feudal organization in his kingdom. Economic circumstances gave him no choice. He could not manage everything by himself, neither the collection of taxes nor the administration. So he had to let his representatives share both taxes and administration, which made them into feudal lords. Instead of fixing our attention on the opposition between king and nobleman, we should rather consider the interplay between their respective developments. For the historical truth is that feudalism was an attempt to establish a new form of national government, stronger than the one that existed before, and it came into being precisely because the royal power was beginning to become a state power. A strong ruler like Charlemagne was just the man to promote the development of feudalism in his domain. The man who completed the feudalization of England was the strongest king the country had had up to that time, William the Conqueror. There is therefore nothing improbable in the suggestion that feudalism in Scandinavia was the outcome of a greatly increased royal power—the Valdemars in Denmark, the Folkungs in Sweden, Sverre and his descendants in Norway. Conflict did not develop until the king and his nobles each began to grasp for additional power—when the feudal lords united into a noble class and wanted to establish state institutions independent of the royal power, or when the king sought a new basis for a more centralized national government. Then rivalry could and did arise between those who previously had been united.

The unifying forces within the state have always been in conflict with forces of other kinds. One of the most conspicuous of these, and always a part of the history of the state, is the conflict between the interests of the state and those of the local communities. This conflict has been given its dramatic statement in Ibsen's play *The Pretenders*. Both forces have some justice on their side, and it has not always been easy to harmonize the two. On some occasions history has even promoted both, but I shall not pursue this theme any farther.

I do wish to call attention to the curious historical dialectics of the situation: the state has promoted ideas of unity that eventually have threatened the state itself. I am here thinking of class feeling and national feeling. Class feeling involves other forces, which I shall speak of in another connection, but the feeling of nationalism is so strongly bound to the state that it teaches us a great deal about the growth of the state itself.

Even though the state was born in war and based on force of arms, it bore within it the possibility for other kinds of growth. It was not always a mere matter of chance how much land could be united into one kingdom. Least of all did the people of those days think so. In their eyes these matters were always in the lap of the gods. It is said that when Harald the Fairhaired "went on land" in Norway and a local chief in the west was invited to join the struggle against him, this chief answered that he did not wish to do so, "for it seemed clear that luck was with King Harald." "Luck" was just such a force outside and above humanity, a divine force. As Homer puts it, "Let one be king and master, he who was ordained by the highest God."

The concept of a unified state therefore centered in the king from the beginning. He *was* the state, and loyalty to him was the first political virtue. The men who entered the service of the king felt that it was their first duty to go to war with him and fall with him rather than yield. This was an emotional factor of tremendous force, one that has fired poets in many countries.

But then the state could grow into something that was above the king as well. For it was a matter of course that the king lived under the laws on which society was founded and which it was his obligation to support—laws that also had divine sanction. As the state gradually grew and was strengthened, it became an independent force, which lived even if the king was gone. Then the subjects became citizens, and the state became a fatherland. The citizens were united by a new feeling of fellowship, which in modern times was called patriotism. We have an abundance of testimony to the existence of this feeling among the ancient Greeks and Romans, even if they had not yet created the word. It was a feeling that made it a duty to give up one's life for the fatherland, one's native state.

When did patriotism become what we now call nationalism, using a still newer word? What is the difference between these two? It is a definition that is not easy to state in exact terms, because it is a question here of feeling. In the first place, the word "nationalism" implies that one's feeling is associated more with the people of the state than with the state itself. Furthermore, there is greater warmth in this new feeling, a warmth that reveals itself in love for the native soil, in joy at living in the native land, and pride at being born just there.

The Greeks were proud of being Greeks, as we often hear, but their pride was turned against "the barbarians" and did not set up distinctions from other civilized peoples. When the Roman proudly declared, "Civis romanus sum," he was thinking first and foremost of the privileges he gained by being a Roman citizen.

Then there is another factor that perhaps characterizes nationalism even more strongly in contrast to pure patriotism. This is the awareness of and the joyful pride in one's national past, one's history. This feeling has found its expression above all in the national anthems. Virtually every one of these reminds the people of the deeds of the past, even if they do not all give such a lesson in ancient history as the Norwegian anthem *Ja vi elsker dette landet* ("Yes, we love this country"). This is something we might call a romantic theme in nationalism, and it is a trait that is more concrete than most of the others.

Of course there is plenty of this pride in the past—one might even call it historical bragging—in the Aeneid, which Virgil wrote at the time of founding of the Roman Empire. But it was not a nation he was honoring: it was a world power. His poetry did, nevertheless, give impulses to the national boasting of later ages.

Scholars who have attempted to uncover the origins and background of nationalism have for the most part derived it from the great French Revolution and from Romanticism. I am convinced that its roots go much farther back, and I have tried to demonstrate this in a paper printed in 1947.[18]

Europe began to organize the separate states that became the core of political life in this part of the world as early as the ninth and tenth centuries. By the twelfth century a lively, independent cultural life had arisen in each of them. This was the period of foundations in the new European culture. In these nations we encounter expressions of new national feelings. They were born in battle and were marked by this fact. They established emotional boundaries corresponding to the political ones.

The most renowned work of nationalistic historical writing in the Middle Ages came from a small people, which at this time was still battling vigorously for its independence—the old British inhabitants of England, the

Welshmen. The author, Geoffrey of Monmouth, a cleric, wanted to hearten his countrymen by reminding them of their noble ancestors. In the middle of the twelfth century he wrote his great work about the British kings. He assured his countrymen that only deception and witchcraft had enabled the accursed Anglo-Saxons to overcome the brave British. He comforted them with ancient prophecies that someday they would nevertheless win back mastery over all of Britain. In addition he could prove to them how much braver and more skillful in battle they were by telling about their great hero, King Arthur, who had subjugated thirty foreign kingdoms, including Scotland, Ireland, Gotland, the Orkneys, Iceland, Denmark, Norway, and all of Gaul, and had even won victories over the Romans and all their vassals. An ancient learned etymology declared that the Britains were descended from Brutus, and in this way they could derive their ancestry all the way back to the Trojans. In a river mouth in Devonshire visitors can still see the stone on which Brutus first stepped when he landed in Britain. Geoffrey padded his story with heroic legends, which became popular in other countries as well, especially in France. Geoffrey's work came to be known throughout western Europe and was even translated into Old Norwegian.

The English were irritated by this Welsh nationalism. A contemporary English historian wrote that Geoffrey was a shameless liar, and he avenged himself by explaining that the British did not have their name from the hero Brutus, but from the Latin word *brutus*, which means "brutish."

The Englishmen of this period had their own national problem in the opposition between the Anglo-Saxons and their Norman conquerors. The problem appears to have solved itself, for in the twelfth century we hear that they could all be called "sons of the same mother." The state was stronger than differences in ancestry and language and provided the best basis for unity and fellowship.

The English stirred up national feelings in another direction also, in France. Here the abbot Suger rose up as the spokesman of French national pride. He described how "all France" flocked to the royal banner in the struggle against the English and German attacking armies, and how universal rejoicing followed their victory. Suger himself, when he died in 1152, was called "father of the fatherland." It was about this time that the old Latin word *patria* began to be used for the whole area under the rule of one king.

In France it is easy to see how this national feeling extended farther than just to the one who ruled the country. We have evidence of this in the great *Song of Roland*, which was composed about this time. Roland, one of the warriors of Charlemagne, became a national hero. In the song that tells about him a good deal is said about national honor and love of one's native soil. The country is constantly called "sweet" or "gentle" France (*dulce France*), a formula that passed into ordinary speech. We have a number of personal letters from a French priest in the 1170's, Pierre of Blois, who used the word in this way, and he tells us what he meant by it. He explains that France is a country without wild animals or barbarians, a country in which it is good to be, a country with gentle air and gentle wines—the land of culture, in contrast, for example, to wild Sicily where the volcano swallows people up.

Because of his love for his own country he could even understand that other people might love theirs, an understanding that was quite rare in those days. In a letter to an English friend who had accepted high office in Sicily, Pierre wrote that he ought to return to England, and gave as his reasons for this: greater security of life, the natural love of one's country, and fondness for the king at home. These are basic ingredients in national feeling.

A nationalistic statesman like Suger did not think in this way. While he said that it was wrong for Frenchmen to obey Englishmen, he found it quite reasonable that Englishmen should obey the French. He expressed particular contempt for the other neighbors whom France had been fighting, the Germans. He described them with an old phrase from Roman days, *furor teutonicus*. He reported how German envoys came and spoke "with German boldness as they grind their teeth." In a less cultured person this contempt could become flippant, like the French knight who said that "even an armed German would not venture to attack an unarmed Frenchman."

The Germans on their side could be just as boastful. But in their country it was not quite so easy to build up a unifying national feeling. They were still split into Saxons, Bavarians, Swabians, etc., and their emperor had very little national power. A poet like Walther von der Vogelweide could still sing in praise of Germany. "I have seen many countries," he wrote, "and noticed particularly the best ones." But his heart was not fond of foreign manners: "German ways are better than all." From the Elbe, the Rhine, and all the way to the Danube he found the best people in the world. And German women surpassed all others: "He who wants to find virtue in pure love should come to our country—may I long be granted to live there!"

Their neighbors did not value the Germans equally. Indeed, it was in conflict with the Germans that the national feeling of other countries sprang into being. In Italy the Germans were regarded as vulgar barbarians and were hated because they were conceited and self-satisfied. The

Italians said that the Germans spoke "with broad jaws," and their language sounded like the barking of dogs or the croaking of frogs. They rebelled constantly against their German masters. Pope Innocent III called upon the Italians to take arms against these "murderers and seducers." Even an Italian poet who fought on the German side let his countrymen ask, "Who can tolerate this German madness (*rabies teutonica*)?" It would have taken but little to turn the revolt against the Germans into full national unity for Italy, but the antagonisms of the different districts were still too strong, and there was no national authority. It was of no avail that new agitators time and again proclaimed the idea of national unity. Italy remained divided for centuries and had to endure foreign masters.

The struggle against the Germans had greater effect on national unification north of the Alps, for example, in Hungary, Bohemia, and Poland. The Polish national movement is particularly remarkable. Here too we find a historian who conjures up a great past for his country. This was Bishop Vincentius in Cracow, who quite evidently modeled himself on Geoffrey of Monmouth. He began to write Polish history at the request of his king, Casimir the Just, who needed such a work. He was battling to protect the independence of his kingdom and to weld his people together. Master Vincentius managed to prove that the Poles were descended from the ancient Greeks, that they had fought with Alexander the Great, and had overcome his successors. Then he told about all the later Polish kings, praised them for their skill at arms, their justice, and their love of country. In particular he boasted about the great Boleslav I, who had defeated the Saxons and subjected to his rule Silesia, Pomerania, Prussia, Russia, Bohemia, and Moravia. He also poured out abuse on the heads of all who rebelled against their lawful king. Loyalty, he concluded, was the king's virtue and the strength of the kingdom. Without loyalty society could not be maintained and man could not live in justice. His book became a textbook in the schools and was widely read. Polish national feeling found its ideals in this book.

Denmark, Germany's neighbor to the north, had some of the same problems as Poland—defense of its independence and establishment of its unity. Here Archbishop Absalon became the national statesman. He named two men to write the history of Denmark, Sven Aggeson and Saxo Grammaticus. Both of them wrote pridefully of Danish deeds in the past. Saxo was the most detailed of them. He too modeled himself on Geoffrey of Monmouth and created a legendary history of Denmark that in one way was even more nationalistic than Geoffrey's. Saxo would not hear of any kind of foreign origin for his people, and he specifically rejected the learned theory that had been advanced by Dudo in Normandy that the Danes were descended from the ancient Greek Danaids. He wanted everything to be purely Danish, and he appropriated heroes wherever he could find them, especially from Icelandic tales, so that with their help he got quite far back in time. He sang the praises of Danish virtues, loyalty and honor, which he contrasted with Saxon deception and faithlessness, and he showed his dissatisfaction with one Danish king who imitated Saxon ways of life. Saxo himself did not invent these ideas; he was giving expression to thoughts that lived in the Danish nobility.

The Danish kings were themselves striving to gain dominion in other countries, in Sweden and in Norway. In Norway they ran up against a national feeling that was just as strong as the Danish one. We meet it in the Old Icelandic saga writers, especially Snorri Sturluson, who in this respect, as in others, was a spokesman for Norwegian thinking. We know his story of the contemptuous words attributed to Olaf Tryggveson in the battle of Svoldr (1000 A.D.). He spoke there of the "frightened Danish goats" and the Swedish "eaters of horse meat, who rather should have stayed at home." But he expected a hard fight from the men of Earl Eirik, the Norwegian rebel leader, because "they are Norwegians like ourselves." It is possible that the story had already been made up in the eleventh century when Harald the Stern was fighting against the Danes, for we hear something of the same boastfulness in verses from that time. It was first written down, however, at the end of the twelfth century, and testifies to the high opinion Norwegians had of themselves at this time. Snorri reports that both Swedish and Danish kings were disinclined to send their men to war against Norway, because they would there meet with a tough and well-armed people. When he wrote his saga of the Norwegian kings, he introduced it by a long prefatory history linking their family to the royal Swedish Yngling family, and in this way he could trace them all the way back through the Old Norse gods to the Trojans in Asia.

In this way the twelfth century brought to Europe a national feeling, filled with a pride that was built on historical memories as well as faith in one's own strength, occasionally even on a superior culture. It is obvious that one of the strongest elements in this national feeling was enmity toward other peoples, particularly one's neighbors. Here was a basic urge to unity—to protect oneself against foreign powers. Therefore the king, the leader of the army, was the central element in the national idea. Words like *patria* and love of fatherland found a place beside loyalty to the king. But war was still the strongest factor in the new concept of unity within the state.

National feeling expanded vigorously during the next

centuries, because the state everywhere developed more and more nationwide institutions. The kings were seconded, not only by the body of councilors in which the highest estates of the kingdom, the nobility and church, dominated, but also by parliaments, composed of estates in which even the lower classes of the people had their representatives. A complex code of laws came into being. National courts were set up, and a national commercial policy concerned itself with general economic interests. People could rally around new national symbols, including heroes of freedom and saints. Then came the Renaissance, which not only revived the ancient classics, but also the national historical writings, particularly those works that had sustained the first nationalism in the twelfth century. Now the art of printing could help to make all national literature available to wider segments of the population. For the middle classes this was a period of economic, political, and spiritual advancement. The national government came to be more interested than before in trade and other economic problems. Mercantilism, with its strong centralization and direction by the state, gained the upper hand in country after country. Its goal was not only economic centralization, but also political and cultural centralization. This appeared in its work on behalf of a national science, of popular enlightenment, and of language cultivation. The development of a common national language became one of the tasks of the state.[19]

Here centralization encountered a resistance born of the problem itself. In virtually every one of the "national" states there were people who spoke languages other than the one that was considered standard. Their "national" language was different from the one the government wanted to give them. In this way the interest in language development created within the state a conflict that stimulated disagreement. There were not many issues that stirred as much fiery enthusiasm and bitter conflict as did the effort to establish new national languages.

There were other and possibly stronger forces that tended to confuse the national situation. These too were forces of union. They included demands on the part of the people for more rights and for "democracy," demands that made many aware of what were called "natural rights." These were going to find their political shape in the doctrine of the "sovereignty of the people."[20] Romanticism transformed this into the "spirit of the nation," which found its chief expression in folk literature and folk language.

In this way the national concept could become a divisive force in the life of the state. The national movements of the nineteenth century wished to establish other borders for national sovereignty than those that had been built up by earlier political forces. In other words: national feeling on a democratic basis became a revolutionary force because it was founded on national traditions that fitted into a new national continuity.

Many attempts have been made to harmonize the two kinds of national unity that have here been discussed. Both carry a powerful freight of deep emotion, and both are living forces in modern history.[21]

In the nineteenth and twentieth centuries we find national sentiment as a force for union in Germany and Italy, for revolution in Poland, and for dissolution of the Austro-Hungarian monarchy. Polish history gives the most remarkable testimonial of how the national will can maintain itself even if the state it was originally associated with is destroyed and subjugated time after time. The feeling that had once been aroused by the state now found its chief focus in the reestablishment of the state.

In Austria-Hungary nationalistic demands could clash in many ways. The Magyars in Hungary were the first to succeed in gaining independence. But they were so strongly imbued with a sense of mastery that they could not and would not consider giving equal opportunities for independent national life to other nationalities within their borders, who collectively were almost as numerous as the Magyars themselves. Just because the Magyars ruled so tyrannically in Hungary, they strengthened the opposition of German-dominated Austria to all kinds of national aspirations, since many of the same suppressed nationalities lived there as in Hungary. In this way the whole monarchy became a raging cauldron of national antagonisms, which finally blew up in two world wars that ended all the unity created by the Empire. Austro-Hungarian history is the most instructive example we have of the force that national sentiment has exerted in modern times.

Nationalism has found a particularly striking form in our own time among the Mohammedan, or as they themselves often put it, the Arabic peoples. Their nationalism is bound up with religion in a way that gives their national sense of unity divine consecration and thereby a psychological strength of quite unusual dimensions. We are still far from having seen the fruits of this development.

The main point in this whole story is the change in the psychological content of national feeling down through the ages. Even though it began as a warlike sentiment that supported the struggle of one people against another, it was gradually colored by the inner fellowship of the people, so that the idea of war had to yield, and among the most advanced peoples even tended to disappear almost completely. In the same way the king became less important as a national symbol, or more correctly, he became nothing but a symbol, while other symbols, for example, the flag, won greater strength in the national consciousness. National solidarity became more important than anything else. This psychological transformation made it possible for national independence to become a natural step towards international cooperation. Many conflicts are still unresolved, but in principle it is clear that they can be ironed out for the benefit of an even wider fellowship.

Chapter V

ECONOMIC FORCES

The Marxist theory of history asserts that economic conditions, the forms of labor, are decisive for the social structure in all countries and all ages. Political and cultural life, it is maintained, assumes its particular form because of the social base that has thus been established. This doctrine gave the economic forces of social and cultural history a larger place in historical research than they had before, which has left deep traces on all historical thinking in later times.

Many believe that Marx wished to attribute all actions and events in history to economic motives. Since he himself called his outlook a "materialistic" view of history, they assume that he reckoned only with material forces. They overlook the fact that his chain of causation is indirect, proceeding from economic conditions through social structures to what he called the historical superstructure. Each result of an economic development becomes a new force in society, which helps to shape it still further. Because of his particular philosophy Marx could call all of this "materialism." But if we follow our usual mode of expression, we will here quite simply see an interplay of all kinds of psychological forces stimulated by economic needs and economic events.

It will be fitting here to quote some words from the first Marxist historian in Russia, Mikhail Pokrowski, with whom I had a conversation about these questions in 1928, at the Congress of Historians in Oslo. After his death he was accused of having been too dogmatically Marxist, for which he was condemned by younger Russian historians. But at that time he said to me, "We must always remember that Marxism is not a philosophical dogma, but a historical method." The method, which consists in digging one's way down through cultural and political life to the economic basis of society, has been used by many who would not call themselves Marxists.

In itself it is clear enough that the material struggle, the maintenance of life, had to be the very first and also the most enduring motivation for human activity. This struggle created the earliest culture, in the effort to make tools that would help man find food and protect him against wild animals and other forces of nature.

Natural conditions have played an enormous role in human progress. Soil and weather, flora and fauna, differing as they did from place to place where men came to settle, made special demands on their adaptability and inventiveness. They stimulated men to use these talents to their own advantage. A new material culture emerged, in which constant improvement of living conditions reinforced social and religious urges in building the earliest societies on earth. These in turn became food-gathering societies of hunters and fishermen, or industrial societies, or agricultural societies, all according to the natural conditions and the state of technology.

In each society the needs were different, and therefore the forms of labor were also different. Tacitus reported that the ancient Germans lived for the most part in separate houses, and he ventured the opinion that this was due to their love of liberty. No one accepts this explanation today; we ask only for the economic or possibly the technical motivation. For that matter, even in Tacitus' day many Germans lived in tightly knit villages surrounded by their fields, and in modern times some historians have maintained that this organization was peculiarly Germanic. But we find plenty of villages in other countries as well, and there were Germanic peoples like the Norwegians who did not have them at all. The Danish historian Erik Arup believed that the village arose when people invented the wheel plow. Its use was in turn determined by the nature of the soil.

In all the older societies that we know there is a division into free men and slaves, and this was indeed a prerequisite of the complex culture that they often attained. When most of the work had been turned over to slaves, or to people who were not much freer than slaves, there was room in society for what Thorstein Veblen called the "leisure class," one that could devote itself to such non-material pursuits as science and art. An upper-class culture was created in which the rest of the people had little or no share.

The most typical, or purest, form of this upper-class culture was the one we find in the colonial cities of Roman Africa. There the Roman army personnel and civil officials lived in complete isolation and left all productive labor to the people outside the towns. On a paving stone in the market place of one of these cities I once saw carved these lines: "Venari, lavari, ludere, ridere, hoc est vivere," that is, "Hunting, bathing, playing, and laughing—this is living." Here we have just the program for a "leisure class." The African upper class produced an emperor like Septimius Severus and an intellectual leader like St. Augustine.

Of course it takes a great deal more to produce a cultured life like this than merely to be free from manual labor. Without this freedom, however, the ancients could never have attained the heights they did, even if perhaps they cut off the roots of progress in so doing.

My special competence does not permit me to express myself in detail about the problems of ancient history. I have noticed that recent research has tended to emphasize economic forces as an explanation not only of the flowering of Greco-Roman politics and culture but also of its decline. My personal studies of the sources in this area are too few and scattered for me to have any independent judgment in these questions.

Only in the Middle Ages do I reach a period whose events I know well enough to perceive the forces actively promoting the historical growth of society. We encounter immediately the organization of society that is the most characteristic of the Middle Ages, namely, feudalism. I mentioned this above in discussing the growth of the state, and I pointed out that political and economic forces cooperated in its creation. There were contributory motivations from other sources, including earlier laws and certain moral ideals of loyalty and honor. The main thing, however, is that a feudal system with fiefs and vassals was to be expected in a state where people lived in a natural economy, that is, one in which each social cell, the family or the village, nourished itself by its own production.

Economic historians have in recent years disagreed as to which part of the Middle Ages really had a natural economy. The Belgian Henri Pirenne, the Austrian Alfons Dopsch, and the Swedish Sture Bolin have taken different sides on this question. Some maintain that it was not until the Carolingian era and in connection with the Mohammedan conquests that western Europe declined into a natural economy. By this time feudalism had already begun to take shape. Others say that this was precisely the period when commerce began to break up the natural economy. It seems to me that there is no conflict between these views. There has always been trade among people; no social organism has ever been wholly self-sufficient. The question is entirely a matter of degree: when does trade become sufficiently intense so that one can say that a commercial society, a monetary economy, has come into being? We must not forget that in the early Middle Ages the amount of trade between countries was very small. The wagons that bore the goods on the roads did not take large loads, and the packhorses carried even less. The boats on the rivers as well as the vessels on the sea were tiny. The quantities of goods that were carried from country to country were necessarily small. We can safely say that in spite of all the changes that growing wealth might bring in its train, western Europe in the Carolingian era was a society whose natural economy could form the basis of political feudalism.

If this is true, we should expect that as trade increased, the feudal organization would weaken. Feudalism had created a strongly decentralized government, but now the government was compelled to become more and more centralized. This is exactly what did happen during the last centuries of the Middle Ages—a little unevenly from country to country, but the direction of the movement was everywhere the same. Forces other than purely economic ones promoted this development. The kings sometimes began quarreling with the vassals they themselves had given authority and tried to take the power into their own hands. Historians have disagreed on whether political or economic motives were the strongest in the transformation we here observe.

It is fruitful at this point to consider the development in England, the first state to be politically and nationally united. We turn to the foremost English economic historian and ask for his explanation. William Ashley, who has written an excellent survey of the organization of economic life in England, does not give a direct answer, for he limits himself to his economic theme. When he reaches the period of the enormous expansion of English trade under Queen Elizabeth, he attributes this expansion to the national spirit that had then grown strong in England. Nevertheless, when we study the movement his work describes, we see quite clearly that economic growth preceded the political and national expansion.

We find that as early as the twelfth century London became the center of English trade with foreign countries, building on an exchange of goods in which wool was the most important article of export. More and more the export came to be centered here from ever larger sections of England. Most of it went to the Flemish weavers on the continent. At first the traders were mostly German merchants, who came and took the wool with them. Gradually Italian, especially Venetian, merchants also came with their vessels. Toward the end of the thirteenth century Flemish weavers moved over to England and began to spin and weave the wool in the country itself. Soon they taught the Englishmen themselves to do the work, and in this way an English woolen industry sprang up in the wake of the trade. The landed proprietors around the country found it to their advantage to produce as much wool as possible, and therefore went in for sheep raising. In this way all of southern and central England was drawn together during the last centuries of the Middle Ages into a common economic life, and an economic unity was built up that bound the people more tightly together. That this was also a transition to a monetary economy appears from the fact that in the fourteenth century the tenants on the estates began to pay their fees in money instead of in grain or other goods.

In politics this development found expression when the citizens of London joined the nobility in creating the Magna Charta in 1215. The citizens were given seats in the national parliament gathered in 1265. It should be obvious that the political-national unity that created these institutions was a fruit of economic unification.

It is also true that the state supported economic development with commercial privileges and other concessions. In this way an interaction between political and economic powers that strengthened both took place. We see this especially after mercantilism came into being in the sixteenth century.

In historical writing it has always been a matter of dispute whether the state or private economic enterprise led the way in the great economic changes of history. One can hardly make an entirely clear separation between these two forces. It was late in the Middle Ages before the state developed any firm economic policy, especially in trade, that included plans to assist the native economy. The economic development itself had to teach the state to adopt such a policy.

We see the same sequence in France as in England. Here, too, it has been maintained that the state came first and that commercial and urban life could not come into being until it had the protection of the powerful political state of about the year 1000. It is a great illusion, however, to believe that the state had any great power in France at this period. For that matter there was no collective French economic life at all in the Middle Ages. The country was divided into two distinct economic areas, northern and southern France, each one having its foreign trade in different directions. This division was reflected in political institutions as well. But the kings made use of citizens from both parts of the country to strengthen their power, and when the great meeting of the estates of the whole country was held in 1302 for the purpose of supporting the king and his national policies, the citizens quite naturally came from all over. Commercial life with its growing emphasis on a money economy was an advantage to the central government. It gave the king new sources of taxation that made him more independent of his noble vassals and enabled him to build up his own military forces.

In other countries economic unity was often much weaker, or even nonexistent. The political development was affected by this difference. Karl Lamprecht maintained that the reason for the inability of Germans to unite into a really effective empire was their economic decentralization. Here the growth of commerce tended rather to reinforce the individual regions, the dukedoms and the counts' lands, or the great city federations, like the Hanseatic League. The regional rulers acquired their financial and military strength from this new economy.

If we follow German history in succeeding centuries, we find that one of its leading traits, one that points forward to a new period, is the tendency of commerce to send its offshoots to the east into the old Slavic countries, to the north along the Baltic Sea, and to the south on the Oder, Elbe, and Main rivers, and down the Danube. In this way new forces of unity were created, and these reinforced the demand for full national unity. Austria and Prussia were the rivals in this struggle. Even when Bismarck finally succeeded in founding the new German empire, there were still many oppositions within it. These were both traditional and economic-social. The strongest was probably the opposition between the landed aristocracy of Prussia and the industrial middle-class society of the Rhineland. Industrialization, however, extended farther and farther. When I wrote my book about Bismarck (1911), I could venture to say that the strongest force of union in Germany then was Social Democracy, which Bismarck had fought so bitterly. We see now, after both the first and second World Wars, that no one in Germany did more for national unity than the working classes.

If we turn our attention to Norwegian history, I think we will find confirmation here also of the importance of economic cooperation for national unity. I have already pointed out the roots of the first national union in the bonds of kinship between nobles in various parts of the country, which made them into an upper class. Such bonds could come into existence because of a growing ease of communication between widely separated parts of the country. This was true above all for the whole seaboard from Hålogaland to Vika, the true ancient Norway, "the North Way." Routes of communication were also opened in the interior, particularly over Dovre between eastern Norway and Trøndelag, and over Filefjell between eastern and western Norway.

We must immediately concede that the bonds of economic interest created in this way could not have been particularly strong, and we see how the political unity of the kingdom was still quite weak. It was not until the twelfth century that economic conditions began to draw the various parts of the country more firmly together. The most important factor in this development was the codfish industry of northern Norway. This yielded a product that formed the basis of regular trade within the country. We hear about ships carrying fish from the North to Trondheim and to Bergen, and soon a place of storage was organized

in Bergen for the exportation of fish to other countries. The
Hanseatic merchants took over this export and made it into
a major factor in Norwegian economic life. Northern
Norway and western Norway were joined together in an
economic unity. It can hardly be doubted that this was one
of the conditions for the new political strength of King
Sverre and his successors, even if this was on a feudal basis.
A short time later eastern Norway also found a product for
export in the timber from its forests.

The East and the West, or as they came to be called, Norway south of the mountains, and Norway north of the mountains, remained separate economic areas for a long time.
This left its traces in politics and produced a deep cleavage
in political life. Not until after Norway had lost its independence were the two major portions of the country
drawn into a common economic life. This was when the
Netherlanders began to buy their timber both in the West
and in the East. It now became possible for a Norwegian
middle class to arise, one that could become strong enough
to initiate a new national policy. In this way economic and
political progress went hand in hand and helped to build
a united Norway.

Even so we know that internal differences could remain
alive for a very long time. I recall that my predecessor in
the professorship of history at the University of Oslo, old
Ludvig Daae, said to me at the time it was decided to build
the Bergen-Oslo railroad that when the line began to
operate and eastern Norwegians and western Norwegians
came into closer contact with one another, they would
quickly notice how different they were. He predicted that
they would begin fighting with one another, just as the
Norwegians and Swedes had fallen out after the railroad
was built between their two kingdoms; and that the western
Norwegians would organize a republic of their own. To be

sure, it was unhistorical of him to say that the Norwegian-Swedish railroad had sharpened the conflict between the countries. The great crisis in this struggle, the dispute over the regency, had taken place some years before. The Bergen railroad, the economic link between eastern and western Norway, was in reality a force for national unity.

In modern times we have another, and perhaps even more concrete example of the force of economic cooperation for national unity. This is the United States of America. The colonies managed to stick together while they were fighting for political independence, though their unity was often on the point of dissolving. After the establishment of the union, the North and the South appeared to be moving in different directions, especially in economic organization. The northern states, which at this time meant chiefly the northeastern states, grew more and more industrialized, while the southern states maintained and even strengthened the plantation system that was built on Negro slavery. It is obvious enough that the economic difference was here also a social difference, and in many ways a cultural or spiritual difference, as well. America appeared to be splitting up into two nations.

The break came on the question of Negro slavery. The northern states, with their economic and military superiority, succeeded in forcing the southern states back into the Union. At first this did not appear to strengthen their cooperation. On the contrary, the enmity of the losers was rather imbued with a new bitterness. The force that was used against them only stirred them up the more. When I was in America on a study tour in 1908–1909, I found that many Civil War memories were still alive, and I saw that a great deal of the old social order was still in existence. The Negroes were still a subjugated and underprivileged class. The master culture, whether for good or evil, was still dominant, and I could even then meet a man who had a thousand Negroes working for him on his plantation.

At the same time I saw that something new was beginning to develop. Close by the same plantation I noticed a tremendous new factory for cotton weaving. In another place I found a whole city—Atlanta, Georgia—that was a regular factory town and looked like a northern city with skyscrapers and everything that went with them. Up to this time the southern states had sold their cotton to the North, or to England, for weaving and preparation, but now they had begun to do the work themselves. They too were becoming industrialized, so that the North and the South were more and more getting to be on the same footing. The difference between them was being leveled out, not only economically, but also socially and intellectually. This unification has continued, until the southern states even could support the protectionism that was the special political program of the North. The time is long past when there could be any question of a new split in the Union.

To me this was a highly instructive situation. The fact that I had the opportunity to see and experience the importance of economic unification at close quarters opened my eyes to similar developments in ancient as well as modern history. More or less consciously we all think in much the same way, as appears from the common use of terms like "state" or "national" economy when we speak of economic questions. We are thinking of the state or the nation as an economic unit that leaves its mark on the political and cultural life of the nation.

At the same time we must be clearly aware that the description I have here given of conflict and unification between North and South in American history is an example of the Marxist method in history. It shows the connection between economic circumstances and social structure, and again between this and cultural life. We must not apply this in an altogether schematic or mechanical way. If we think through the psychological events in question, we will quickly see that economic conditions do not directly or by themselves become the causes of a will to unity. Their effect is first and foremost that they bring into being the possibilities for unification. They foster a fellow-feeling that may become the starting point of a will to unity. Many other factors can strengthen this trend and shape its character. They would have little or no force, however, if the economic basis for unification were not present. It is an appreciation of this connection that is the true Marxist method in history.

I once made an attempt to apply this method in greater detail in another area of history. This is the problem of the origin of the European and especially the Italian Renaissance. We here meet one of the greatest and most discussed questions of world history, which is the reason for its being so instructive in our discussion. For a hundred years this period has been a central problem in historical research, and many different solutions have been proposed. Now it is obvious that a phenomenon as complex as the Renaissance can not be accounted for by any single explanation. Historians have therefore concentrated on the factor that seemed to them most important, most unifying, in this movement. This is the new *individualism* that emerged in so many fields of life and society. Some have emphasized the political fragmentation and conflicts in Italy, others the religious uprisings that were connected with the heretics and the Franciscans. Some have attributed it to the Italian national character, others to the character of the Germanic invaders of Italy, the Goths and the Lombards. Some have thought of the Renaissance merely as a natural development from the older culture of the Middle Ages. Most of these explanations apply only to Italy and do not really suffice even for that country. We need an explanation that will account at the same time for the Italian origins of the movement, and for its spread throughout the rest of western Europe. The first historian who pointed out the economic backgrounds of the Renaissance was Karl Lamprecht, but he discussed only Germany and the new capitalism in that country.

My own contribution was to turn to the economic causes in Italy herself. I discussed it for the first time at a Scandinavian historical congress in 1920.[22] Since that time I have worked with it at various times and discussed my views both in Norway and abroad.[23] What has given this work a firm basis is the fact that there is scarcely any portion of the world's economic history that has been more thoroughly investigated than that of Florence. It is quite obvious that the Renaissance first emerged in Florence and found its capital there. One need only mention names like Dante, Petrarch, Boccaccio, Giotto, Masaccio, Donatello, and hundreds of others.

Florence was the place where commerce and industry first broke away from the old guild system and developed an industrial capitalism built on personal initiative. The masters of this new industry were not the old craftsmen in their shops, but the capitalists who hired people from many different crafts and set them to work in the production of textiles. Among these were people who carded, spun wool, dyed, or performed other operations that helped to transform the raw wool into fine clothes. This was a tremendous technical-economic revolution, which took place in the last half of the thirteenth century. We can follow the development towards individual freedom in the economic field in laws given from 1289 on. The new freedom led to economic competition and conflict, and in its wake came a liberation in the fields of culture as well—in art, poetry, and science. The old guilds were no longer autocrats dominating handicrafts and art, but organs of the political authorities who could protect the freedom of the artist. The chronological connection seems clear enough—first economic liberation, and then social and intellectual liberation. The psychological connection is equally clear: the artist worked his way up from being a member of the guild to being a free worker. The spirit of individualism won a place throughout the whole social order.

The developments in Florence were repeated in other places, first of all in the other Italian city-states. There is a striking parallel in the Dutch industrial towns also, where economic freedom was followed by the Flemish Renaissance. Capitalism and the Renaissance go hand in hand on all sides. Here is a historical development that only the Marxist method seems to account for in full.

As we have already suggested, there are other motivations as well behind this great movement. The new study of Greek and Latin literature has its roots all the way back through the Middle Ages, but now the classics were used to strengthen spiritual freedom in religion and philosophy. Influences from Byzantium also participated. National movements strengthened the sense of a national past. But the all-important background is the new economic life that made the middle class the leading cultural force.

This explanation is not, however, entirely adequate for France. Here the Renaissance was mostly sustained by the nobility. It was primarily a fashion among the French nobles, which kept it from bringing with it the same widespread cultural liberation as in other countries. In French architecture and painting the art of the Renaissance was for the most part imported. The explanation is perhaps not too difficult to discover. French art had already had its great breakthrough in Gothic architecture. We find in Normandy a special development, which we might call a kind of national Renaissance, in which the church builders turned back to the old Romanesque style. In Norway this kind of national awakening is the only aspect of the Renaissance we know.

The new economic life of the Renaissance was followed by a still more radical economic revolution, which transformed the social and intellectual life of Europe. This was the Industrial Revolution, the employment of machinery in production and communication, which began in England in the second half of the eighteenth century and gradually extended its mastery to the whole world.

Many historians have looked on this revolution as a fact that needed no explanation. The new machinery represented a great technical change, and these historians felt that their task was to describe the consequences of this change on society, and after that on other areas of human life. Some of them said straight out that the inventions themselves were due to chance. I could not feel satisfied with this conclusion, which I read in the writings of a prominent American historian while I myself was living in America, the great land of the machine. I decided to investigate the origins of the great technical inventions. I found some of the materials for this research in the Harvard University library and the rest in the British Museum. I arrived at an explanation some twenty-five years ago, which I felt made the whole development completely understandable.[24]

It is almost a matter of course that the motivations were economic. As in Florence during the Renaissance, the textile industry called forth the new inventions. It was not as in Florence, however, the woolen industry, but the processing of a new product, cotton, which came from the new colonial countries. This was the stimulus to new activity in the mother country. It was a question of producing cheap goods in great quantities, a mass production of products that were in ever-growing demand. The question of how one could meet this demand was a crucial problem. I discovered that producers and other interested persons made great efforts to find better implements than those they already had, implements that would work faster and produce more. Year after year they organized societies and offered prizes, and they received numerous proposals for new constructions, until finally some came that were successful. Man's inventive capacity was placed at the service of economic needs that themselves were also human enough. There was a kind of circulation between two aspects of man's mental life, but point of departure and goal were both economic, so that it would be hard to find a better illustration of what is meant by economic thinking in historical research.

My discoveries about the new inventions of the Industrial Revolution led me to think about other inventions that had left their mark on history. I connected them, for example, with researches I had made earlier into the origin of Gothic architecture. I had studied various old churches where there were evidences of certain features from the Gothic style, even though the churches otherwise were built in the Romanesque style. I then realized that the old architects had been experimenting with innovations that might meet certain needs of the service or of the congregation. In this way they found their way to a new technique, one that was more functional than the old.

I thought then of all the inventive techniques of our own day, of how rationalized they have become, and how technology leaves nothing to chance. But experimentation, which now is the major feature of natural science and technology, was not entirely unknown in earler ages either. Later developments can thus often throw light on earlier ones. Here, however, we find other motivations besides the economic ones. The interplay of forces in social life has become more and more complex.

The mechanical inventions of the eighteenth century opened the way for a whole flood of technical discoveries, which in truth revolutionized the world. They multiplied the production of goods and have never ceased to do so. They multiplied the exchange of goods in the same way. The whole world and all its people were driven into an economic cooperation where money was king. It was an expansion that broke down all barriers and demanded a free path for trade and economic enterprise. No one can overlook the psychological and political connection between the new economic liberalism and the general spirit of freedom that became prevalent. It looks like chance, but there is a deep connection in the fact that the free trade program of Adam Smith's *Wealth of Nations* appeared in 1776, the year of the American Declaration of Independence. Liberalism was not merely an economic program; it stamped its image on politics and culture around the world. Individualism became the unifying trait of the nineteenth century.

It is an interesting fact that in our own day, when social life seems more complex than ever, we nevertheless perceive the economic factors more clearly and vividly than people did earlier. It is quite natural that Karl Marx should have been born in this period. He and his teaching are a product of this economic-social life, just as much as Darwin and his "struggle for existence." Many are now inclined to see economic motivations in everything that happens, especially in politics, foreign and domestic. It is clear that there is plenty of economic causation in politics, especially in the kind of politics that is called "colonial."

Since colonialism has played so large a role in the conflicts of the major powers in our time, we tend to apply the same concept to all struggles for power.

Perhaps we should pause a little before dismissing other kinds of motivation that have been advanced for colonial policy. In the beginning, especially, there was much talk of religious motivations, the idea of bringing Christianity out to the poor heathen. We hear about this when the Spaniards sent their ships over to America and subjugated the West Indies, and when the Portuguese began sailing southward along the west coast of Africa. Was this pure hypocrisy? I do not think so. The Spaniards, especially, made serious efforts to Christianize the Indians. Dominican and Franciscan monks, and even more the Jesuit missionaries, built up great Christian societies on American soil. Because he saw that the Indians were being ruined by working for their Spanish masters, the great apostle of the Indians, Bartolomé de Las Casas, worked for the introduction of Negro slaves from Africa. The Christian evaluation of all human beings as equals before God did not, however, appear to play any great part in the lives of these Negroes.

Even if Christian missionary activity was a central concern of the representatives of the Catholic church in America, it is still undeniable that the governments regarded it as of minor importance, and the secular colonists paid even less attention to it. These were all interested in exploiting the natural resources and the work force of the newly discovered countries to the greatest extent possible. They did so without any notable consideration for the natives. An enormous economic advantage accrued in this way to the ruling countries of Europe. Those countries that did not succeed in joining this exploitation tried to get their part of it by whatever means they could—by piracy, war, or the colonization of areas which were still available.

All of this had a far-reaching effect on European history and on world history—an effect that was economic, political, and cultural.

I do not intend to discuss this further, for the facts are well known. I only wish to point out how the economic motives that stimulated colonization were still vital factors of decision in the development of these areas down to the present time. They determined the way in which the colonies were ruled; they shaped the lines of economic policy; and they stimulated the great colonial wars of the seventeenth century and later.

It can probably be said that colonialism first made economic motives dominant in foreign policy. There had been wars before for purely commercial reasons, especially wars that were conducted by economic units like the German Hanseatic League. We know this especially well from Scandinavian history between the thirteenth and sixteenth centuries. We can also demonstrate that the stimulus to the great Hundred Years' War between England and France in the fourteenth and fifteenth centuries was economic rivalry between England and Flanders. But purely political problems of power quickly entered, and it seems likely that competition for power has been the leading force in creating wars between states.

It probably applies to many modern wars also, that they are due more to a competition for power than for economic gain. In many cases political and economic motives are so strongly intertwined that it is not easy to distinguish them from one another. This applies to the struggle for such "spheres of interest" as the various great powers demanded for themselves in various parts of the world, especially in Asia and Africa. We have seen in recent years a similar fierce competition for the oil lands of Western Asia.

The greatest influence of economic conditions in international politics is not so much the stimulus they have given to competition and war as the difference they have brought with them in the balance of power between the great powers. The most conspicuous fact here is that the powers which predominated at the turn of the twentieth century—France and Great Britain—have now been reduced to the second rank. Their place has been taken by the two young unions, the United States of America and the United Soviet Socialist Republics. Here it is quite obvious that economic conditions have determined the new constellation of power.

France and Great Britain issued victorious from the two World Wars of the twentieth century, but they lost economically what they had won on the battlefield. Great Britain had had a central position in the economy of the world down to the time of these wars. The wars impoverished her so tremendously that from being the greatest creditor in the world, she now became a debtor, while the United States at the same time changed in the opposite direction from a debtor to a creditor country. Before this time Great Britain had been able to live on capital invested in countries in all parts of the world, but now it was in debt to other countries. The old English colonial areas developed into independent states and carried on their own politics. England could tie them to her only by giving them lower import duties on their products than on those of other countries. They accepted this, however, more as their due than as a gift. Great Britain was no longer the unchallenged spokesman of the British Commonwealth of Nations.

In France the development was more complex, for here the decline had begun a long time earlier. Here there was a visible economic stagnation as far back as the first part of the nineteenth century. The great Industrial Revolution

of the eighteenth century, which made England an economic power, had relatively little influence in France. One
important reason for this was, of course, that French soil
contained so little of the iron and coal that were the foundation of the new English industry. France remained to a
great extent an agricultural country. Then there is the
remarkable fact that the comparatively large population
which had made France the greatest power of all until the
beginning of the nineteenth century, remained almost
stationary, so that it fell behind the population of one
country after another. It is obvious that the population in
a country is in itself an economic factor, besides the fact
that it has a direct influence on military strength. What was
it that stopped the growth of the French population?
Social scientists have debated the question a great deal,
without being able (as far as I can see) to give any wholly
satisfactory answer. The motivations may be psychological
and social, as well as economic.[25]

We see that the French became a people of economizers
more than any other people in the world. They were a
hard-working people, but their universal hope and dream
was to be able to retire and live comfortably on the means
they had saved. They never ventured to put their savings
into enterprises that would produce new jobs and in time
possibly yield great returns, but in which there would
always be an element of risk. They lived by a rule that even
got into their textbooks in "morality," namely, that a small,
certain interest on money is better than a large, uncertain
one. When they did not quite simply hide their savings in
their chests or in their famous stockings, they placed them
by preference in state securities, domestic and foreign.

In any case, capital was in this way withheld from
industrial production. Their economizing also led naturally

to the practice of limiting one's family to two children. As far as the French peasants were concerned, the reasons for this might go back to the great Revolution. This event had promoted liberalistic conceptions that led to a constant partition of French farms among their heirs. The system spread, however, to the citizens as well. When population did not increase, there was no growth either in the labor market or in purchasing power. There was little need for new enterprise or new production. As early as 1819, a French economist could write, "We have no need of so many machines, for labor is cheap with us."

In this way a deplorable reaction was set in motion in French social life, a vicious circle: reduction of the birth rate, therefore small increase in production, therefore new decline in the population growth, and from this again more stagnation in production. Under such circumstances the many wars with all their destruction of manpower and capital had to have even greater effects in France than in other countries. It became extremely difficult to get the country back on a sound footing. France inevitably became less and less of a great power, losing its colonies and having to seek help from other powers.

The end of the matter was that only two really great powers were left, America and Russia. Of these two Russia has made an especially noteworthy advance in economic strength and population. I shall speak of this separately in another connection.

International developments like these have forced us to pay more attention to economic questions than our own domestic situation alone would warrant. Nowadays our people have many interests, but we still notice how easily economic ones come to occupy their chief attention. We have grown accustomed to looking for the economic backgrounds of the events around us. This makes it easier for us to understand the way in which they have influenced the history of the past. Historians have, of course, shared in all that has occupied the thoughts of their contemporaries. They have learned from their own time. This is a part of their obligation.

Chapter VI

CLASS CONSCIOUSNESS

The class struggle is an important part of Marxist historical thinking. The main thesis of the Communist Manifesto of 1848 is well known:

> The history of every society down to our own time is the history of the class struggle. Free men and slaves, patricians and plebeians, proprietors and peasants, masters and apprentices, in short, oppressors and the oppressed, have been in constant opposition to one another and have carried on an incessant secret or open war, which always has ended in a revolutionary transformation of society, or in the common destruction of both classes.

It is obvious that the idea was here exaggerated for propaganda purposes. For one thing, it applies only to pure social history. For another, it does not in reality say anything more than that always and in all societies there have been upper and lower classes. If in any period the "war" between them was "secret," this is really to say that at that time there was no war. The lower classes were satisfied with their condition. In addition, the whole history of society was here simplified beyond all reality. For the most part there have been intermediate classes between the uppermost and the lowest. The upper classes could be split into various layers, which might even be in competition or at war with one another. The lower classes that rose in revolt might be on their way to becoming an upper class themselves. We need only think of the plebeians in Rome; their leaders were wealthy men who were felt to be just as good as the patricians whose power they wanted to usurp.

In spite of all such reservations, the doctrine of the class struggle was still a fruitful historical idea. It clarified for us the tremendous historical importance of class cleavage. It taught us that the history we read is to a great extent upper-class history only, written by and about the upper class. It conceals a life below the surface, a set of emotional attitudes that are associated with economic conditions.

This last point, the psychological aspect, is one I would like to dwell upon. It is, to tell the truth, rather obvious, except of course that older historians paid no attention to it. The condition of all class struggle is that there must be a *class consciousness*. We are clearly aware of the existence of this feeling in daily life, and we need only project it back into history to see the force it has had. Perhaps we should call it a *consciousness of rank*, for it is most strongly associated with the prestige one enjoys in society. Here aspects other than the economic play an important part, even though the economy is the basis and the starting point. We meet this consciousness as pride of class, and we discover at the same time that class feeling arises first in the upper stratum. It does not rise into history from below, but for this very reason it can call forth a spirit of rebellion in the lower classes and arouse class conflict.

A group pride of this kind quite naturally finds expression in a sense of unity within the class, and this feeling may be in conflict with other social loyalties. We find an expression of this in the class consciousness of the nobility in the Middle Ages. We know that those who had been admitted to the nobility felt themselves to be internationally united. They had an obligation, as it were, to help one another. They gathered at the same kind of games and enjoyed them together, and they had a whole world of poetry of their own. Arthur, Tristram, and Parsifal were their heroes in all the countries of western Europe.

Much of this bore a merely romantic aspect. It could, however, turn into politics, a politics that might endanger the state, if the nobility should find that it had economic and political interests beyond the national borders. This was true in the last centuries of the Middle Ages. The same nobility that had been one of the main pillars of the state now became a major foe of national power and unity.

We have some evidence of this in an important event in Scandinavian history. I have suggested that this is the true origin of the Scandinavian trend towards political union at the end of the Middle Ages.[26] I felt that it was impossible to be satisfied with the explanation given by Kr. Erslev, according to which Queen Margaret pursued her policy of union because of a tradition she had inherited when she was married into the Swedish royal family of the Folkungs. This family, he maintained, had furnished the leadership in a policy of union between Norway and Sweden. I felt that much broader presuppositions for the idea of union could be found in the social and political conditions of the Scandinavian countries, and that Margaret had simply exploited these. It was my suggestion that the impulse to such a policy came from Denmark. There we find the first serious strife arising between the royal power and the feudal nobles. When a powerful fraction of the nobility was outlawed for the murder of the king in 1286, its members asked and got help from their peers in Norway and Sweden. In this way a cooperation sprang up among the Scandinavian nobles that continued through many vicissitudes in all three Nordic countries. The cooperation was strengthened by intermarriages that created common economic interests through property holdings across the borders. In this way one could more and more speak of a pan-Scandinavian nobility. Margaret succeeded in winning the support of this nobility. She defeated the Swedish king in battle in 1389, but even before this she had a strong party of Swedish followers. She was not slow to make agreements and promises that were designed to win over the nobility.[27]

What makes this policy of Scandinavian union the more remarkable as a testimonial to a general development of the period is that we find parallels to it in other European countries.[28] The greatest similarity is to the Polish-Lithuanian union of 1386. A powerful Polish nobility succeeded in establishing a union with Lithuania on condition that the nobility would gain extensive privileges on Lithuanian soil. It was not many years before the nobility of the two countries was completely united.

In other countries the conflict was more intense. In Scotland there had been from the twefth century an immigration of Anglo-Norman nobility into the English borderlands, and even into the Scottish lowlands, so that this part of Scotland was completely feudalized. In 1288 a Scottish parliament, in which the immigrated and native nobility joined hands, decided to unite with England. The "maid from Norway," granddaughter of the late Scottish king, was to be the link between the kingdoms. She was to marry the English crown prince, who was a grandson of the same king on his mother's side. The marriage was never consummated because the "maid from Norway" died on the way to Scotland. Then the Scottish nobility fell out, and it took three centuries for the Scottish-English union to come into being. Eventually it was the Anglicized Scottish nobility that made it possible.

We find similar developments on the Iberian peninsula. There, too, the noblemen moved easily from one kingdom to another until a common Spanish nobility gradually came into being. This furnished the background for the general Spanish union of 1469.

At the same time German nobility was spreading out in all directions: into the Danish Schleswig, the Czech Bohemia, and the Wendic countries of the Baltic. The nobility brought these areas under German domination and provided the continuing leadership in all the shifting trends toward a union of Bohemia, Austria, Hungary, and Poland in the fifteenth century. On all sides we find a political policy dictated by the expanding power of the nobility.

Within the class politics of the nobility we observe also a great deal of inner competition. All power politics is by its very nature strongly selfish. No one wishes to give any bit of power away to others. We see the effects of this clearly enough in Scandinavia, where the Swedish nobility split off and at length separated entirely from the Danish. We see it in Scotland, and in the relations of Poland and Hungary. In its very worst form we observe the internal cleavage of the nobility in France in the Hundred Years' War, and in England in the Wars of the Roses. In these cases the conflicts became a powerful threat to the existence of the states themselves. The new national states had to be built on social classes other than the nobility.

In the period when the nobility was at its highest power, the lower class that was under its immediate rule and therefore the most exploited, that is, the peasants on the nobles' estates, rose up in revolt. In the last centuries of the Middle Ages we hear of peasant uprisings throughout Western Europe—in England, France, Germany, and Denmark. It is an interesting fact that sayings and slogans from these uprisings passed from country to country and stirred up the peasants. It is not strange that the uprising of the Dalecarlians under Engelbrekt in Sweden could strike fire in Norway also. It is somewhat more surprising that there is a connection between the Hussite wars in Bohemia and the Swedish revolt. Among peasants in Setesdal in Norway we meet with slogans from the uprisings in Germany.[29] The revolt of the lower classes that began in this way was unorganized and yet quite extensive. It was everywhere struck down by force of arms, and the peasants were worse off than they had been before.

As it turned out, it was not this class that would put an end to the power of the nobility. That was reserved for the urban middle class, which rose up and pushed the nobility aside. The "citizens" were a part of the new monetary economy and had gained strength by virtue of their great capital resources. In the early Middle Ages the social structure was reflected in a little verse about the three estates: the pastor says, "I pray for you," the nobleman says, "I fight for you," and the peasant says "I work for you." There was no room for the merchant in this scheme, and even less for a capitalism built on money. The merchant's enterprise was actually regarded as being outside the moral world. The church considered it a sin to take interest on money, and not until the end of the Middle Ages was this prohibition abolished. By that time the bourgeoisie had become so powerful a force in social life that the merchant's morality had to get the blessing of the church. More and more the citizen class entered into the highest councils of the state. The king employed the citizens as a counterweight to the nobility and strengthened his authority with their help. Or perhaps one should turn it around and say that the citizens made the royal power an instrument of their interests.

We can find an example of this in the introduction of the absolute monarchy in the kingdom of Denmark-Norway. During the sixteenth and seventeenth centuries the middle class in both countries had gained more and more economic power in the state. The citizens felt a pride of class that imbued them, especially in Denmark, with a consciousness of their own power and a consequent distaste for the authority of the nobility. A nobleman is said to have asked one of them if he did not think there ought to be a difference between lords and peasants. To this he replied, "We are not your servants." This will to self-assertion emerged at the meeting of the estates in Copenhagen in 1660. The kingdom was in economic and political hot water after its severe defeat in the war with Sweden. The citizens' estate under the leadership of Burgomaster Hans Nansen won the support of the clerical estate under Bishop Hans Svane, son of a burgomaster. Together they compelled the nobility to yield up its privileges, and they freed the king of the restraints the nobility had laid upon him with their electoral privileges and special charters. They succeeded in making the monarchy hereditary. There were radical plans that aimed at depriving the nobility of its power over the peasants, but such ideas were rejected. The issue at stake was the power of the state itself, and this was achieved by the charter giving the king full sovereignty and absolute authority.

The decisions taken in Copenhagen were in effect decisive for Norway as well. Yet the charter was later submitted to the Danish nobility, clergy, and citizens for confirmation, and just so, it was confirmed at a meeting of the estates in Norway also. Here it became even more evident than in Denmark that the purpose of the new form of government was to confer the real authority on the meetings of the estates, especially the citizens' estate. The citizens united in support of proposals for their own class interests, primarily economic ones, but also sought such privileges as access to all positions that previously had been reserved for members of the nobility.

In both of these respects it proved that the introduction of absolute monarchy was a victory for the citizens. The economic policy of the state became a mercantilism intended to protect national trade and industry. Citizens now entered into all government offices. This was to some extent concealed by the fact that many government officials with a bourgeois background were ennobled. The purpose was to give them titles just as fine as those of the noblemen who were to the manor born. But it did not make them any less bourgeois, for they were not given grants of land, which formed the true basis of the power of the nobility.

The development in Denmark and Norway was duplicated throughout Europe. The period of absolutism was, in fact, the period of growing bourgeois power.

This is not to say that the power of the nobles was entirely broken. Even if the nobility was no longer dominant, it did have great economic privileges, since the great landed properties remained in its possession. Even here it was losing out, however, as citizens acquired more and more of those lands, and the noblemen themselves became economically dependent on the wealthier citizens. They still maintained a group solidarity, which expressed itself as a consciousness of status rather than of class, after the failure of their economic basis. In many countries we find a numerous but impoverished nobility with little left of the old privileges except its titles and its pride. When this nobility still insisted on asserting its power and demanded the respect of the lower orders, it made itself into a public spectacle like Don Quixote, or the character in one of Holberg's comedies called *Don Ranudo* (read backwards *o du nar*, "Oh you fool"). This nobility could collapse at one blow, as it did in the French Revolution.

"The Third Estate," the class of citizens, made its entrance on the scene in a famous pamphlet by the Abbé Sieyès (1789). The third estate, he wrote, wanted to be something, but should in reality be everything. Such a demand was actually presented at the great meeting of the estates that called itself the National Assembly. The demand was met when the two other estates moved over to the third and were absorbed by it. The policies of the Assembly were determined by the third estate, as is seen in the important resolution of August 4, 1789, which proclaimed that the feudal order of society should forthwith be abolished.

The demands made by the oppressed French peasants on the nobility were in reality much more radical. They had a far less marked class consciousness than the citizens' estate. But they had not won any real power in the state, as had the citizens, and for them much greater economic interests were at stake. They bore the real burdens of the old feudal system, and they gained the most from the abolition of that system. They now succeeded in throwing off all the old feudal privileges and taxes. They were able to free themselves by purchase from those taxes that were not actually abolished. It was a tremendous victory for long-standing demands on the part of the peasants.

The class struggle of the peasants was not yet over. Those very principles of freedom that were asserted by the citizens in the Revolution created new economic difficulties for the peasants. I am thinking, for example, of the unfortunate consequences of excessive subdivision of the farms, as mentioned in another connection. Yet the class struggle of the nineteenth and twentieth centuries in France and other European countries was not to be initiated on behalf of the peasants. Other submerged classes presented their claims and started the conflict that gave birth to the Marxist doctrine of the class struggle. This was primarily the class of industrial workers. Before discussing this, I would like to say a few words about the special form of class struggle that found expression in the so-called "farmers' movement" in Norway. We have here a unique combination of the basic elements in that struggle.

In my book on the farmers' movement (1926)[30] I dated the start of this conflict to the years around 1500, when great changes took place in the economic life of the country. Then, and throughout the sixteenth and seventeenth centuries, we can safely say that the Norwegian farmers were a lower class, working on soil they did not themselves own. Their work was for the benefit of various kinds of landed proprietors, mostly the nobility. This was equally true of land owned by the state, whether rented by noblemen as a fief or otherwise. The farmers revolted against the many new taxes imposed on the land, and this gradually turned into a demand for the right to own the land itself.

It has been objected that this could not be called a class struggle, since the farmers were not united. It is true that the revolts took place within the local regions, or sometimes even in single communities. Their demands, however, always concerned more than just a single farm. The farmers wished to maintain what they considered to be the ancient laws of the land. They sometimes declared that they would unite with their fellow peasants throughout the country, or even in the whole world, in a revolt against bailiffs and tyrannical landlords. In the 1670's "supplications" came in great numbers from all parts of the country, demanding that the king should expropriate, even without restitution, all the lands he had recently sold to noble or bourgeois proprietors. In some places the farmers offered to redeem the property themselves. This was so general that it must have been the result of widespread agitation.

Then came the great change in the farmers' situation. Economic and political circumstances towards the end of the seventeenth century made it possible for them to buy more and more of the farms they had been cultivating. In this way the number of freeholders increased enormously during the eighteenth century. The farmers' movement might still have as its aim to restrict the ownership of land to the farmers, but now an upper class had come into being among the farmers themselves. Their purpose in the struggle was to gain all possible civic rights for themselves on the same basis as the previous upper classes. The spirit of this struggle found expression in the proud reply that a wealthy farmer in Ringerike made to an officer who claimed privileges because of his rank: "I, too, belong to a nobility!"

It is striking to see how deeply this struggle affected the thinking and outlook of the farmers. As early as 1905 I took up the problem of describing their rebellious mentality, as this found expression in all kinds of local folklore and other oral traditions.[31] This was an entirely new way of looking at these materials. The main point was that through them we could trace a long-standing spirit of rebellion, which became a force in the farmers' movement well into the nineteenth century and later.

My purpose in writing the book about the Norwegian farmers' movement was to show that the agrarian politics of modern times was not based on great political principles. The principles were born from and fostered by a struggle whose purpose was to win for the farmers a power and economic independence that would keep them from being exploited by other classes of society. It was a struggle born of economic circumstances. I suggested that this century-long struggle had firmly implanted in the farmers a vivid sense of justice that sparked the great conflict of later centuries. The farmers believed in their rights, and would fight to gain them.

A Danish historian who was critical of the Marxist approach objected that I was inconsistent in reckoning with psychological forces in the class struggle. But I have never dreamed of excluding the demand for justice as a driving force in the class struggle. On the contrary, I regard the craving for justice as a fundamental trait of human character. It can stimulate people in other social classes to aid the rise of a lower class because of indignation at what they consider to be injustice. Among those who suffer the injustice there may arise an involuntary need for self-assertion and a will to resist the violators of justice. These are basic traits, and they belong as a matter of course in every revolt of the lower classes. The problem is only to learn which conditions in society awaken these feelings and make them into dynamic forces in history. Primarily these are economic conditions. In my book on the Norwegian farmers' movement I tried to show that time and again changes in economic circumstances forced Norwegian farmers into struggles and more struggles. I even proposed to trace in a purely chronological way a connection with the changing prices of agricultural products imposed by conditions abroad.[32]

Similar agrarian uprisings formed part of the background of the French Revolution. We know them from other countries as well. The characteristic thing about the Norwegian farmers' movement was that in its last period it turned against a class that in most other countries was still struggling for its privileges. This was the estate of the citizens and the civil servants, which in Norway had become the only upper class. The only other place in which a similar situation can be found is in the New England states in America, where Shays' Rebellion of 1786 was a clear counterpart to the Norwegian Lofthuus Revolt in the same year. It was put down by force of arms, but had, nevertheless, great political consequences, especially in the psychology of American farmers.

Then, finally, came the last great class struggle with the rise of the labor movement in the nineteenth century. This became the greatest of all class movements, since it united the workers not only in whole countries or states, but, through an international organization, in the whole world. I do not need to outline this movement in detail, as it is well known to all. Everyone has had personal experience with it, and it has entered into daily life in all possible ways. Not until this movement came did it dawn on most people—or let me rather say, on historians—just what class struggle meant for the growth of society.

The new revolutionary working class was a creation of factory industry. Before this time it might often look as if the workers and the masters in an industry stood together in a single social class. Saint-Simon at the beginning of the nineteenth century was the first to describe history as a transfer of power from one social class to another, with the power moving most recently from the nobility to what he called "the industrial class," the citizens' estate. This class seemed to him to be an unbreakable unity, with common interests for all who belonged to it, whether of high station or low. The historians who followed in his wake, for example, Thierry, Guizot, and others, wrote their histories in this spirit. They were the historical interpreters of the citizens' class, and to them this class was "the people."

The Industrial Revolution brought with it a new view of society and of history. The "industrial class" was broken up, with conflicting interests contending for control. The social life and thinking of the public were influenced by this new struggle, as was the thinking of historians. Marxism took shape and saw the class struggle in everything that took place. The great year for the emergence of the new workers' movement in various European countries was 1848, which proved to be a turning point in European history.[33]

In Norway this came at the height of the farmers' movement, which embraced at once agrarian politics and peasant romanticism. The farming class was actively engaged in an assertion of its own rights in opposition to the old privileges of the citizens. The farmers also stirred up cultural controversies by asserting their rights to a language based on their speech rather than on that of the cities. Folk art and folk poetry contributed a new and refreshing color to art and literature. The movement stimulated a view of history according to which rural society had been the great link of unity between Norway's past and present.

After 1848 the labor movement drove a wedge into this ideal rural society, which had seemed to be adequately represented by the landowning farmers. These latter had sent their men to the *Storting* and had demanded new economic and social privileges for themselves. After 1848 it was discovered that behind and below these champions of peasant liberation there was a lower class of cotters and other agricultural workers, who did not share and were not supposed to share in the new freedom. These formed the backbone of the first Norwegian labor movement under Marcus Thrane.[34] This movement split the agrarian political group and shocked the whole people. It represented a transition from romanticism to realism.

All the labor movements of 1848, including the Norwegian one, were suppressed. The main thing, however, was that now a new class solidarity had been created, one that became a growing power in every country. It took the form of a new kind of conflict, one involving wages and leading to strikes. It called forth new forms of law, such as the collective wage contracts that came to be protected by laws and courts. It gave birth to a special legal code relating to labor, regulating the conditions and hours of work and providing state insurance against accidents, illness, and unemployment. A transformation of the whole social structure was set in motion.

The idea I particularly want to pinpoint is the development that resulted from the growth of class solidarity itself. I could not help noticing very early that any class struggle that entered politics generally dressed itself up in a framework of general principles. The politics of the third estate in the French Revolution led to the proclamation of the universal, natural rights of man. The agrarian political movement in Norway transformed itself into a leftist movement with liberalism and democracy as its slogans.[35] In the same way it was natural for the labor movement to establish as its goal a principle of social policy. This was found in socialism.

Socialism took many different forms of a practical and theoretical nature down through the years. In the beginning it was often strongly utopian and sought to outline both the framework and the content of a new social order. Karl Marx taught the workers to take a more historical view of the path that should lead to the new ideal society. As the workers advanced on their way, and the social conditions around them changed, the practical forms of socialism had to change as well. Above all, labor policy had to be transformed into general social policy.

In this connection I pointed out as early as 1910 that we could find in Norwegian history a constant progress towards national unity through the rise of successive classes.

Norway was born when the nobles united to rule the country. This rule of chieftains transformed itself into feudalism and thereby became a danger to national independence. Then a middle class grew up into national solidarity, and in 1814 it took over the leadership in the movement for independence. Then came the rise of a rural class, which proved to be a powerful factor in promoting national unity. The labor movement was still in its infancy. It was my conviction that as it advanced, this movement would also promote a fuller and richer national solidarity. There was a kind of historical dialectics in this: through constantly renewed struggle and division toward greater unity, from class solidarity to national solidarity.

The development I felt could be demonstrated for Norway was found in other countries as well. I may remind the reader of how the third estate became the National Assembly of France in 1789. I proposed that this development be regarded as a general law in a lecture at the International Historical Congress in Oslo in 1928.[36] Among those who supported my position was a spokesman from the Ukraine.

My prediction for Norway has come true as time has passed. It has been confirmed, for example, by the change of what was once called "labor law" into social policy. The insurance that first was called "worker's insurance" has now become a national insurance. In the beginning the Labor party rejected all nationalistic issues in politics and culture as something that concerned the middle class alone. Gradually, however, they incorporated these issues, and in some cases, as in the language conflict, could even hoist a flag of union over the field of battle. The standard of living of the laboring classes has been raised to such an extent that we have a noticeable spreading out of prosperity in such matters as housing, clothing, or food. This development has led to a decreasing emphasis on class conflict. The problem is now one of general social policy, which after due discussion has been more or less completely put into effect.

Chapter VII

REVOLT AND OBEDIENCE

When I was in school, we were told that there were two contrasting types of people in ancient Greece, the liberty-loving Athenians with their lively, creative culture, and the severely disciplined Spartans, who obeyed their authorities and lived in spiritual stagnation.

When I later read the verses on the Spartan memorial at Thermopylae, I got an inkling of the fact that there could be something of a personal will, something great, even in the Spartan submission to an almost inhuman discipline:

Traveler, go and report to our people at home in Lacedaemon: Here we have found our graves, obedient to their law.

In my student days, when the struggle for Norwegian independence filled our thoughts, and we learned that it might become necessary to take up arms for our cause, I eagerly joined in the singing of the "March of the Girondists" from the French Revolution, which concluded with these words, "The most beautiful and enviable fate of a man is to die for his fatherland." The Athenians, too, were willing to fight, both at Marathon and at Salamis. Were there really two different kinds of people in Athens and Sparta?

If we consider the world and its history, we find an abundance of examples of people—individuals, nations, classes—who have meekly bowed down before the orders of their masters, or submitted themselves to the circumstances in which they were born. Even so we see that time and time again there have been uprisings among them. We know that even a dog that has been trained and whipped into complete obedience can be provoked into such rage that he will bite. Are things any different with human beings? Does there not live in their inmost hearts a wish, which can become a determination, to follow their own ideas and their own desires?

There was a time when the greater part of mankind actually consisted of slaves, whose spirit was so cowed that they bore their fate without complaint from generation to generation through thousands of years. During all this time they did precisely as they were told. Then one day Spartacus came to them and urged them to rebel, and the result was a dangerous war of slaves. Spartacus himself was not born a slave; he was a prisoner of war. Yet he did succeed in stirring up tens of thousands of men who were born in slavery, but who risked their lives for freedom, fired by a new determination.

If we consider everything that has been called "class struggle" in history, we find that the lower classes have always needed considerable time before it occurred to them to revolt against their masters. We need go back only a century or so to find a time when the great majority of working people considered it right and natural that they should live in poverty under the domination of wealthy masters. They believed that God had so created society, and this they had to accept. The idea of revolt came to them from people outside the laboring class. They themselves had to attain a certain measure of knowledge and independent thinking before they could unite on any program of deliberate assertion of their rights. The school laws of 1869 were one important prerequisite for the labor movement in Norway, since they introduced secular knowledge into the public schools, which had previously imparted nothing but religious training. It was no mere accident that the typographers were the first to organize labor unions, for they were closest to book knowledge.

Christianity played a curious role in this matter. Christians made it a moral principle that one should not resist evil but be submissive to authority. At the same time Christianity proclaimed that one should obey God more than men, or, in other words, follow one's conscience. There was a double consequence of this. On the one hand it could lead to a purely passive resistance, so that Christian believers might become martyrs. Out of this martyrs' blood, however, could grow a spirit of rebellion, a will to active resistance. As it turned out, the demand for obedience was the Christian doctrine that had the least success. It never won the upper hand among the peoples of Europe.

The great Christian philosopher Thomas Aquinas, who became the teacher of Catholic Christendom both in social and theological matters, taught that subjects should be obedient to those whom God had instituted as their authorities, but not to those who had revolted against God. To be sure, Holy Scripture proclaimed that "all authority is from God." When the authorities, however, refused to do the will of God, they no longer had their authority from Him. Such rulers earned for themselves the name of "tyrants" in a Christian sense, and the people had the right to oppose them and revolt against them. On the basis of this reasoning Pope Gregory VII released the German subjects of Emperor Henry IV from their duty of allegiance: the emperor, he claimed, had been disobedient to God. In this way the right of rebellion became a religious duty and might even become a part of the law.

In the old Norwegian law of the Frostathing one paragraph (IV, 50) reads:

No man, whether a king or anyone else, shall make an attack on another man. If the king should do this, a call to arms shall be sent around in all the districts, and the people shall go against him and kill him if they can lay hands on him. If he should escape, he may never again come back to the country. Anyone who refuses to join the attack against him shall pay three marks, and so shall he who stops the call to arms.

At about the same time as this was written in Trøndelag, Snorri Sturluson in Iceland wrote his romanticized story about the controversy between Lawman Torgny and the Swedish King Olof. In this story the lawman says to the king, "If you will not make peace with the king of Norway, we yeomen will attack you and kill you, for we will not put up with your warlike and illegal acts." Even though the speech is probably fictitious, it testifies to the mode of thinking at the time when Snorri was writing.

It is clear that on this point there was agreement between the new Christian law and the old pagan one. It was the king's first duty to preserve peace and justice in the land. This was his promise to the people when he accepted the throne. If he himself broke the peace and the law, he had sinned both against God and the people, and he had forfeited his right to the kingdom.

The same idea could arise, though with less severe penalties, if the king made himself guilty in other ways of injustice to any of his subjects. It was then possible to call the king before the court and prosecute him. We have a much-discussed story from twelfth century Norway about such a case against a king. The most important part of this is not the subtle interpretation of the law and the legal trickeries that the sagas enjoy describing, but that the king was subject to the laws and could be judged by a court of law. This has its root in ancient legal practice, as well as in the Christian idea expressed by the church father St. Augustine: "If justice disappears, what more will the nations be than vast nests of robbers?"

This reasoning eventually led to the establishment of political safeguards to prevent the king from committing injustices. It found expression in the English Magna Charta of 1215, where it was decreed that the barons could temporarily take over the rule of the country if the king should be guilty of violating the law. In Denmark the royal charters gradually set up more and more safeguards against the abuse of royal power. We see a growth of this kind in one country after another, until it developed into the doctrine of the sovereignty of the people.

The conflict between royal and popular power in the organization of the state will not be entered upon here. It is sufficient to have pointed out the basic psychological motivation of this political development. I shall only mention one specific expression of the psychology involved, namely, that the right to resist tyranny could be used to justify the murder of tyrants. The moral basis was established in ancient times with the murder of the Athenian tyrant Hipparchos in the year 514 B.C. In later times his murderers were celebrated as semi-divine heroes, and the word "murderer-of-tyrants" came to be a term of honor. Even Christians could find such action moral and honorable, as in the case of the ardent Catholic who considered it a good deed to kill the apostate French King Henri IV in 1610. The tradition is alive in our own day: the memory of the men who tried to kill Hitler in 1944 is still being honored.

When we praise such an act, we do so because we judge it primarily by the motives that inspired it. We involuntarily feel a sympathy with moral revolt. This has been a driving force in history in every age and in many different ways.

In the eighteenth century, when the struggle for complete political and intellectual freedom seriously began in Europe, some held that the spirit of freedom had been roused by the peoples of northern Europe—the Germans, and especially by the "purest" of them, the Scandinavians. To some extent this notion was founded on a description of the Germanic peoples by the Roman writer Tacitus in his *Germania*. Later research has shown that Tacitus had a polemic purpose in his description: he wanted to hold up to the Romans an example for them to follow. Therefore we no longer take quite literally everything he tells us about the freedom of the Germanic peoples. In the eighteenth century there were again good reasons for holding up a similar model to the people. After that came romanticism with its doctrine of the national spirit that characterized each people or nation. This fitted in well with a belief in the Germanic spirit of freedom. Historians thought that one could find this spirit in the attacks of the Germanic tribes on the Roman Empire and also in the Viking expeditions of the Scandinavians.

The French Protestant historian Guizot, who wrote shortly before the July Revolution of 1830, described the barbarians of the period of folk migration as typical individualists. They were driven, he said, by a passionate desire for personal freedom and love of adventure. These Germanic barbarians, he claimed, introduced the spirit of intellectual freedom into European civilization and thereby reinforced the old demands for economic freedom raised by the citizens. He found this new spirit also in the feudal system when it was founded. He believed that feudalism was built on a voluntary association of man with man. It was natural that he, as a Protestant, should consider the sixteenth-century Reformation as the most important development of that period. He saw in it a tremendous victory for the spirit of freedom, for independent thinking, for the liberation of the mind from the compulsions of authority. It was not just a reformation, a reform of something old, he believed, but in reality a revolution. Where did this revolution win its victories? Guizot said: In Germany, Denmark, Netherlands, and England—all of them Germanic countries. The conclusion had to be that it was the Germanic spirit of freedom that in this way showed its strength.

Later historians have not been willing or able to accept this chain of reasoning in its entirety. We no longer believe that the spirit of freedom characterized the folk migrations. Still less do we believe in the personal spirit of freedom in the feudal system. We are quite willing to accept the idea that those who initiated the Reformation were motivated by a desire for freedom, but we see few signs of spiritual freedom in the Protestant states that broke away from the papal church. Luther and Calvin both turned against all rebels in a harsh and irreconcilable spirit. In the Protestant churches there came to be just as much religious compulsion as in the Catholic countries. No freedom had been achieved, and in this respect the Germanic were no different from the Romance peoples.[37]

If we are looking for a spirit of freedom among the early Scandinavians, we must first consider the idea that the Norwegian migration to Iceland after 870 was a flight from the intolerable tyranny of King Harald the Fairhaired. Those who interpreted this movement as expressing a love of freedom in the folk spirit of Norway forgot the implication of this idea, namely, that all Norwegians who did not migrate must have lacked this love. These actually constituted a majority, both of the chieftains and of the people. The idea was derived from the writings of Snorri Sturluson in the thirteenth century. But in reality he could offer only a few examples of people who had left Norway because they were at odds with the new king. One cannot generalize on so narrow a base. When we see that members of the same family, even brothers on the same farm, parted company, some migrating while others stayed at home, it becomes impossible to believe in a spirit that characterized the whole nation. We see, instead, differences among individuals, not among races. This applies to the whole course of Norwegian history, as well as to Danish and Swedish.

Protestantism actually had its roots in the uprisings of Christian heretics in the earlier Middle Ages. These uprisings broke out particularly in Italy and southern France, as discussed above. All of them were born from man's universal will to revolt. No one can doubt that there lives in the human mind a deep-seated urge to fight against anything that one feels to be unjust or oppressive. It may begin as a purely personal battle, born of one's desire to assert a personality. From this it can expand into a joint struggle on the part of a whole group of people, a class, or even a nation. This urge is the source of all struggles for freedom and of all revolutions in history. Economic, social, or political circumstances may constitute the background for such a struggle, and thereby provide it with causes and a goal. But it is the human will itself that has to be stirred up and given its force before any rebellion or revolution can occur.

We know revolutions in the ancient and in the medieval world, some that succeeded and some that failed. The introduction to a whole series of revolutions in modern times was the uprising of the British colonies in North America in 1776 against the mother country England. This furnished us also with a remarkable example of the wedding of the spirit of rebellion with the urge for cooperation.

The American war of freedom is sometimes classified along with the many national movements of Europe in the nineteenth and twentieth centuries. This is not correct, for the American revolt was not the upsurge of an oppressed nationality. It is sounder to say that the revolt itself was what made the colonies into a nation.

The only valid comparison would seem to be one with the liberation of Norway in 1814. Here, too, there was little national will before the uprising, and if Norway had not been forcibly parted from Denmark by the great powers, many years might have elapsed before Norway broke out of the union. It is true of Norway as well that the uprising of 1814 was what created the Norwegian nation.[38]

We must grant that there were some preparations for national feeling in Norway before 1814, as there also were in America before 1776. But it was the struggle for independence that transformed the urge for cooperation among the colonies into a national will.

The American Revolution had its roots, not only in economic differences between the motherland and the colonies, but also in a living spirit of rebellion among the people of the colonies.[39] The majority of the colonists who took part in the Revolution had come from England and had inherited from there a tradition of self-rule. Those who had migrated to the same colonies from France, the Netherlands, and Germany, also had various traditions of freedom behind them. There were abundant psychological backgrounds for revolt, which were reinforced by the agitation for freedom throughout Europe in the eighteenth century.

The factor that triggered the Revolution was the English policy of governing and exploiting the colonies for the benefit of the mother country. This was, after all, the reason the colonies had been established in the first place. As the colonies gradually built up an independent economy, they found it more and more irksome to be treated as wards. They were irritated by English interference in the form of police regulations and tax assessments—all of which stemmed from the colonial policy. This policy offended their economic interests as well as their will to independence. Therefore they decided to revolt.

The fact that it was the English colonists themselves who led the uprising against England demonstrates how little there was of national feeling in it. The French in Canada who had been forcibly subjugated by the English a mere twenty years before did not lift a finger. This became a war of Englishmen against Englishmen.

The old English colonies were divided into thirteen distinct provinces. War with France and with the Indians had forced them together so that they had become accustomed to consult with one another, and now they united in a compact of war against England. It is important to note that the people of the colonies were not at all unanimous in their support of the Revolution. In reality the revolutionaries were only a minority. American scholars have calculated that about one-third of the colonists were rebels, another third were loyalists who opposed the Revolution, while the remaining third were indifferent and were ready to join the victor. This is true at least of the thirteen colonies taken as a unit. The proportions might be different in each individual colony, and it was of the highest importance that the Revolution probably had a majority in the two large colonies of Massachusetts and Virginia. The main factor, however, was that the revolutionaries had the best organization and the most effective slogans in their agitation. They had the necessary determination and could win the rest to their side. The core of this party was made up of the descendants of Englishmen, including those who were called Scotch-Irish and who were mostly from Ulster in northern Ireland. In any case we have here a vivid testimonial to the fact that people who might otherwise seem to be quite homogeneous could be both revolutionary and non-revolutionary.

In a great Declaration of Independence the colonists now proclaimed the reasons that had caused them to revolt. They wanted to prove to all the world that they had a right to rebel. They portrayed the English king as a tyrant who himself had forfeited his right to be king. In fact, they claimed, he had deposed himself, so that now the citizens were free to organize the government according to their own will. They were basing themselves almost word for word on the political philosophy that John Locke had propounded in defense of the English Revolution of 1689.

A few years later came the Bill of Rights, which proclaimed the universal rights of man and were supposed to apply to all the peoples of the world. This was a list of all the rights to freedom that Americans and Europeans were going to be fighting for during the next century and more. It was the basis of all the revolutions that followed, above all the great French Revolution of 1789. These human rights were more than just a theory. They were an expression of feelings, wills, and demands that lived in the minds of men and cried out for realization in life. Liberty, equality, fraternity became the battle cry of the century.

An English historian, Richard Cobb, has recently attempted to portray the psychology of an ordinary revolutionary.[40] He has made a special study of "the spirit of revolution" in France, notably in the year 1793–1794, when the Revolution reached its climax under Robespierre. The sources of his analysis are diaries, letters, and newspapers. The results of this investigation are in certain respects different from what most people would have expected.

Those who led the Revolution were people who called themselves, and were called by others *sans-culottes*, or "long-breeches." This term expressed their opposition to the nobility, who were elegantly dressed in the knee pants of the day. Opposition extended not only to their clothing, but also to their customs and their way of life. This was the only social philosophy of the men of the Revolution. One should notice that, contrary to Karl Marx, they did not make any distinction between masters and apprentices. Both were regarded as equally good *sans-culottes*. As a matter of fact, most of the craftsmen who took part in the Revolution were masters rather than apprentices. It was the same in the army: the active revolutionaries were the non-commissioned officers, not the privates. This shows that the Revolution was in many respects a good middle-class enterprise. Except for their opposition to the nobility, the thinking of these men was not in any way socialistic. Cobb makes this clear by pointing out that when they were asked who was a true *sans-culotte*, they did not inquire about his class, but they asked if he had the right opinions. The important thing was the party and not the class.

How, asks Cobb, could the true revolutionary demonstrate that he *had* the right opinions? He had to love liberty, and he had to love his country. He had to be a burning patriot, for foreign powers were exerting themselves to suppress the Revolution in France. The revolutionary therefore had to be a model in his society so that the Revolution would gain respect. He had to be skillful in his occupation, a good husband and family provider, and live a spotless life—or in other words, fulfill all the moral ideals of bourgeois living. Everyone had to stand together for the sake of the Revolution. No one was allowed to distinguish himself by any peculiarity, either in his speech or in his dress. It was a form for equality that resulted in a pressure for uniformity. All of them were firmly convinced that they would win the victory for their ideals. They relied on their party leaders, believed in them, and obeyed them. They drew from these leaders whatever knowledge they got about their country and the world. If the leadership of the party happened to change, they willingly went along and changed from the old to the new. If old party leaders were deposed, or even executed, they immediately and without opposition condemned those whom they had recently hailed and acclaimed. The party was everything.

Anyone who reads this description by Cobb of French revolutionaries can hardly fail to be struck by the number of traits which we here seem to recognize from the Communist Revolution in Russia. Then it strikes us that something must be lacking here. There has to be a faith in victory and loyalty to party in every revolution. The will to raise a revolt, however, to take the first step, has to have something more of passion and fire in it. Once the revolution has been established, one can be content with the more solid qualities, a firm spirit of patience. The beginning has to be elsewhere. It is one thing to make a revolution; it is quite another thing to defend it and build it into the life of a society.[41]

Let us now consider the events that took place in Norway in 1814 and 1905. Both occasions began with a forward surge of passionate idealism. Afterwards there had to come a clear-headed appraisal and a systematic establishment of the essential principles of the struggle. Many felt this period as a disillusioning comedown, and historians have spoken sometimes of these events as defeats rather than victories. Such a development is, however, quite natural. We are dealing here with two quite different psychological situations and two kinds of ability.

In either case, however, we see a remarkable harmonization of elemental rebelliousness, or will to liberty, with an equally strong determination to yield obedience to the leaders. The National Assembly at Eidsvoll in 1814 was concluded with a promise and a handclasp to stand faithfully together. The spring of 1905 united everyone in severe discipline. This was not felt as involving any self-contradiction, which brings me back to my first suggestion—that the people who demand freedom and the people who bow down in obedience need not be two wholly deviant types. Obedience may even be a fruit of the will to freedom.

This brings us to another question: can the revolution itself change human personality? This is something one may dream about, but there is absolutely nothing to support the idea. Frenchmen are assuredly the same now as they were before all their revolutions. Utopian descriptions of future socialistic societies sometimes appear to take it for granted that the people living there will be better than they are today. But even a fully established socialistic society need not ask for qualities in their members other than those they already have. It is only that the new circumstances of society may give the old basic qualities new orientations and new modes of expression. Perhaps there will no longer be any need for the will to revolt? Who knows—it may find expression in quite other fields than in the social one. It is deeply anchored in the mind of man, and all attempts to impose uniformity may lead to a revolution against the revolution. This, too, is something we may dream about.

Chapter VIII

THE ADVANCING POWER OF THE STATE

Everyone has observed how institutions created by man's urge to cooperate have themselves become forces in private and social life. Even within man's narrowest circle, the family, children are indelibly stamped by their experiences. Modern psychology has given us deep insights into this early influence on the emotional and intellectual life of the child. When children leave the immediate circle of the home, they are exposed to a multitude of influences from the new society they have thereby joined. They are compelled to learn what they ought to do, and what they ought not to do. Society has its own morality, which inevitably demands more or less uniformity. The individual and society may come into conflict, but even the nature of this conflict is determined by the society within which it occurs. Society irresistibly shapes its individual members according to its own laws. The many are nearly always stronger than the individual. Ibsen's thesis that "the strongest man is he who stands alone" is valid only when he is really alone and has no one else to contend with. The hermit can rule his own kingdom. But in any society, great or small, even the most absolute monarch is shaped by the social forces that encircle him.

I shall take up for special consideration the one of those social institutions that in our day has developed into possibly the strongest force of all. This is the state. It is most instructive to observe how the state has acquired its dominance within the historical period. Indeed, "the historical period" begins with the state. Everything that precedes the state is prehistoric. For this reason it is not strange that the state has come to fill most of the space in textbooks of history. To a great extent they have been written by the state itself. When historians try to find space for other topics in their textbooks, it is part of the struggle *against* the power of the state.

We have seen earlier (p. 65) how the state was founded as a military force under the leadership of kings, whose function it was to defend their country when it was at war with other states, or even to subjugate other states under them. Soon the kings had to begin taxing their people in order to maintain the armed forces, besides mobilizing them to make war. Since the kings also were entrusted with the maintenance of domestic peace, they had to strengthen the judicial authority that society had established to provide peace and justice. In the earliest Norwegian laws there was no judicial authority other than the one exerted by the great assemblies called *things*. Yet the very earliest kings from Harald the Fairhaired on were praised by the bards because they punished thieves and robbers. During the following centuries judicial authority was concentrated more and more in the hands of the king and his servants.[42] Power was being centralized in the state. The same thing was happening in other countries also, in one way or another.

As the state gradually drew more and more areas of social life under its dominion, it happened time and again that competitors arose who also wanted power over men. One of the most important of these was organized religion. To be sure, this applies only to Christianity and the Christian church. In classical times state and religion were so intimately joined that they made only a single power together. Religious life was not at any rate organized into a central power that could compete with the state. The codes of law were often held to be of divine origin. This was the case with the Mosaic code among the Jews. The Mohammedan state also issued from a religious movement, and its Koran was as much a secular as a religious code. State and religion remained indissolubly joined in all Moslem countries. For this reason religion became the most important element in the national movements of these countries. It became a Mohammedan nationalism, not Egyptian, or Syrian, or Berber.

Christianity was different. It grew up outside the state and often in conflict with the state. The organized Christian church became a power of its own and helped to lead Europe forward into the new era which we call the Middle Ages.

In calling the church a "competitor" of the state, I am using the word in its original meaning of something that moves together with, or alongside of, and is therefore in cooperative rather than in unfriendly opposition. After Constantine the Great had made Christianity a state religion, the state took over the task of building the Christian church. The state called the great church councils, and the state determined what the true Christian doctrine was going to be. The state gave the church power within its own borders.

This intimate collaboration between secular and religious authority proved to be permanent in that empire which called itself Roman, but which we usually call Byzantine. In western countries the development was different. Charlemagne tried to restore the Roman Empire in the West, and as I have mentioned in another connection, he proclaimed that he would rule his empire according to Christian principles. It proved, however, to be impossible to keep all of western Europe united under the Roman emperor. The result was that in western Europe state and church came to have different limits. The church asserted the unity of all Catholic countries at the same time as these were politically dispersed into many distinct states.

This did not immediately interfere with cooperation between the church and the heads of state. An entirely erroneous view, which often has been expressed in modern historical writing, is that the church was constantly attempting to take over secular authority and push the state aside, or even to become its master. Among Protestant historians, and later among the positivists, one will find the advance of the church described as "aggression" against the state, and an expression of ecclesiastical "arrogance." This is a projection back into an earlier period of experiences and events from those later ages when conflict had arisen between state and church. The Norwegian historian J. E. Sars protested against this kind of anachronistic historical writing as long ago as 1856. I have myself tried in various connections to show that throughout the early Middle Ages state and church lived in complete harmony. I have been able to demonstrate that when kings accepted their countries as a fief from a Christian saint, such as St. Peter,

St. Dionysius, or St. Olav, they often did so in order to protect the independence of their country.[43]

Actually, the church was at first only concerned about establishing Christian law and morality in areas with which the state at that time was not concerned, for example, in marriage. Even heathen barbarians had their marital morality, but marriage, the life together of a man and a woman, was not subject to any public law. The church imposed a variety of rules and regulations, such as the requirements of consecration and sexual purity, prohibitions on marriage between close relatives, and severe punishments for all violations of these new laws. Another area was aid to the poor and the infirm. The church succeeded in establishing a tax, the tithe, which was used, among other things, for helping the poor. The church built hospitals for those who fell ill. It was a matter of course that the church had to provide for instruction in Christianity, and even if common schools were not immediately established, there was at least a beginning. Proper schools had to be founded for those who were to be priests; in this way higher education came into being. These activities provided a vast field of operations for the church, a whole array of social activities directed by the clergy. I need only mention such additional fields as church architecture and art. We are here concerned only with the social institution of the church and the power it came to wield.

There were periods when state and church got into conflict, for example over judicial authority. As the church developed a stronger organization, it demanded the right to punish its own servants and to mete out justice, even for ordinary secular crimes. Not all kings were willing to accept this extension of its authority. The church also wished to reduce the power wielded by the state in choosing the bishops of the church. In the eyes of the kings, the worst presumption of the church was its claim to the right of deciding whether a head of state was a tyrant, a rebel against God. It was by this authority that Pope Gregory VII excommunicated Emperor Henry IV, and that Pope Innocent III did the same to King Sverre of Norway.

In this way clashes arose between state and church that involved both principles and power. The relationship between state and church was debated in learned treatises. One of the earliest of these was one that King Sverre caused to be written shortly before the year 1200. This document was rather less theoretical in its approach than many of those that followed it. Intellectual weapons were thus employed in the battle, but they were not the only ones. The church, of course, had no others, while the state could also employ the force of arms and politics. In the end the state won out.

The decision came with those events that we customarily unite under the name of the Reformation. We think here first and foremost of the countries that broke out of the Catholic church and established a creed that made certain changes in Christianity. The program of reformation, however, which demanded that both "head and limbs" of the church should be "reformed," extended far beyond the so-called Reformed countries. To a great extent it was effected in Catholic countries as well, by a drastic reduction of the authority of the church.[44] All along the line, the church was defeated as an institution of power. This defeat was, of course, greatest in those countries where the church was converted into a state church and thereby became an organ of the state. Only one of the reformers, Calvin in Geneva, tried to build up in his state a kind of theocracy, a rule of God, where state and church were one. English Puritans later tried something of the same, in

England as well as in America. In either case, the end of it was that the church fell under the domination of the state, or at least lost all of its political functions.

The conflict between church and state was not thereby ended, either in the Protestant or in the Catholic countries. The church was anxious to win back what it had lost. This was one of the primary purposes of the new order of Jesuits. A time was to come when lovers of liberty adopted the cry of Voltaire, "Crush the infamous one!" (*Écrasez l'infame!*) The "infamous one" was nothing else but the church itself.

In most places the conflict arose over the schools. Secular schools had been established during the last centuries of the Middle Ages—universities for advanced education and schools for elementary education in the city-states of northern Italy and the Netherlands. In the modern period the governments of all countries began more and more to organize such secular education at all levels of teaching. The state and the church were often at loggerheads over the mastery of these schools. The bitterest strife broke out in France in the nineteenth and early twentieth centuries. Again the state carried off the victory, in spite of a variety of compromises.

At the same time as the state took away the power of the church, other innovations developed in its activity. The change was not due to any single factor. In the early Middle Ages the formation of the Christian church and the break-up of the Roman Empire had both characterized the new era. Now there were, in addition to the religious reformation, the new explorations and the tremendous advances in seafaring and commerce. European life was transformed, and the state became a leader in establishing policies of trade and colonial expansion.

The state had not been entirely without economic interests even earlier, but the political leadership had mostly been concerned with the income and the expenses of the state itself. These purely financial considerations did not leave the rulers much time to think about the prosperity of their people. It did occur, as we remember from the speech that King Sverre gave in Bergen in 1186. He was driving out the Germans, he said, because they came with wine and enticed people to drink so that there were fights and murders. He also disapproved of their exporting butter and fish from the country, for these were goods the people ought to consume themselves. But he thanked the English and people from Norwegian possessions in the Western Isles because they brought to the country useful goods, such as flour and cloth, honey and wax.

Now it is obvious that the Norwegians could not obtain the kind of goods they really needed without selling some of their own production. Butter and, even more, fish soon became the great exports of the country. The kings that followed Sverre made trade agreements, especially with the Germans, to promote such commercial transactions. These proved to have a very great importance for the economic life of Norway in the centuries that followed. In such trade agreements the kings had an opportunity to show at least some consideration for the interests of their subjects. They were most concerned about preventing foreign merchants from supplanting natives in *domestic* trade. They did not consider the importance of keeping the *export* trade in Norwegian hands. This was because the main concern of the kings was the excise taxes on ships and goods, which they needed for the national treasury.

Only in the small city-states of northern Italy, Germany, and the Netherlands were the governments compelled to think of measures for promoting the native economy. The German cities learned that trade meant power, and they exercised it by using blockades as weapons against foreign governments that would not let them have their way. The Hundred Years' War between England and France in the fourteenth century was largely caused by disagreements over the Dutch wool and cloth trade.

In this way economic questions began to enter politics. It was not until the sixteenth century, however, that they became one of the central concerns of rulers. It quickly became apparent that trade with the new countries in America and East Asia required the backing and protection of the state. Any territory that the state wanted to exploit had to be won by force of arms. This period of colonial expansion led to an entirely new theory of the state, the doctrine of mercantilism. This theory declared that it was a major concern of the state to strengthen the national economy in every possible way. The state became an instrument of the economic interests of its citizens, particularly those who were engaged in trade and in production for export. The middle class seized power in the state and centralized its government more and more for the promotion of economic advancement.

Rapid and extensive centralization characterized the mercantilistic state. As the number of new enterprises expanded, the state felt a need for more and more servants. The state became a state of bureaucrats, who built roads and canals, abolished internal tariff barriers, organized public postal services, and surrounded the country with a network of customs offices. The state established trade concerns and industrial enterprises and often invested great capital sums in these. The concerns were given monopolies as a kind of state institution. Now that the interests of the citizenry came to be paramount, the state began to organize public schools that were built not upon Latin, the book-language of the church, but on the language that was being used in government offices. All the schools were to have a common national language. The unity of the state was the law in all areas, to the detriment of local peculiarities. The fact that the king could say, "I am the state," was due to the fact that he was the hub of its centralization. The actual rulers, however, were the civil officials.

After all this regulation and regimentation came the inevitable reaction. The middle class grew so strong that it wished to manage by itself and to free itself from the dominance of the state. The state had helped to give it strength. Now that it had come of age, it rose against the state and demanded freedom. Liberalism replaced mercantilism. Later on, demands would be raised for national protectionism and other aids to the native economy. This, too, was an expression of economic growth.

I will not pursue this story any further. I merely wish to point out that a multitude of organizations rose up to become new competitors of the state. The world entered into the era of what was long called "associations." These were economic and professional organizations of all kinds —societies of traders and craftsmen, workers and farmers, political parties of all shades, discussion clubs and societies for self-improvement—societies without number for all kinds of interests, material, intellectual, or even physical. Some societies made it their goal to solve certain social problems that the state had not yet taken up, such as the care of particular groups of handicapped people.

In the period when the fashionable cry was for liberty, the liberty of association was one of its demands. The old state did not approve of private organizations that had greater aims than purely social intercourse. It frowned on all organizations that were not regulated by the state itself, as were the craft guilds, for example. These guilds were targets of the liberals, who wanted to substitute their own free associations. The new societies were in principle voluntary, but people could be forced into them because of the power the societies had over certain branches of industry, or certain political parties. They could develop a power that even defied the state, as appeared when they organized strikes, or lock-outs, or boycotts.

The policy of the state in this situation could not be one of suppressing such organizations, but rather to try to incorporate them into the state itself. This was the program that socialism developed in various forms. The earliest socialists dreamt about the possibility of escaping both the state and the private economic organizations by building up small independent cooperative societies. This proved to be entirely utopian, as it was usually called. The associations had to find their place within the state.

This has become the task of the twentieth century. The most significant innovation was no doubt the many kinds of social insurance that began to be established in country after country from the 1880's, which have expanded more and more as the years have passed. The state has also given subsidies to many other kinds of social welfare. Such subsidies have inevitably led to state control, which has been established in one area of social life after the other. Everywhere we find an organized cooperation between the government and private organizations, particularly in economic life. In our own country of Norway this is true of the production of power and of aids to agriculture. The state has assumed a plethora of new duties, one of the most important and successful being the duty to provide work for the entire population. The state has developed from being merely a judicial state to what we now call a welfare state. We ask that it shall employ its power for the promotion of happiness among all people. Even more, the state has become an instrument for new economic enterprise, a true driving force in progress.

The socialistic program was most systematically adopted by the Bolsheviks in the Russian Revolution of 1917. Here the transition to new forms of society was more sudden and vehement than in any other country, because there had been so little preparation in private economic life and in general popular education. The Revolution was accomplished by a tiny minority of determined and disciplined Communists. This is one reason why the new economic structure has required such harsh control over the people.

There is another aspect which is even more remarkable. Karl Marx had prophesied and taken it for granted that in a socialistic society the state would be replaced by an economic organization of the workers. Henrik Ibsen had written that "the state has its roots in time; it will reach its climax in time," and then fall. Instead we see now in Russia a more strongly centralized state power than we know from any other period. In a purely organizational sense it is characterized by the fact that the rule is in the hands not of the working class, but of the party. There is only one party, on the plea that since there is only one class in the country, there can be no economic conflict. According to Marxist theory, the party cleavages of other countries are due to the opposition between upper and lower classes. The state is therefore an instrument of the one party, the Communist party, and is in reality all-powerful. Those who in any way oppose the party are enemies of the state and can not be tolerated. It is obvious that the state is then compelled to educate everyone in the correct party line. The party has to give instructions on how scientists and poets shall think, and it can use the power of the state to see to it that this requirement is enforced. The question is only how long it will be possible to maintain such intellectual repression.

If we turn from this society, with its communistic principle, to the society that most strongly maintains the opposite principle, the American one of the United States, we meet here also a state that is constantly growing and expanding. It is the only democratic country where the state at one time actually opposed the social demands that were being added to the functions of the state in Europe. When citizens in some of the individual American states wanted to establish social laws, their efforts were time and again declared to be unconstitutional. In the end this interpretation of the Constitution was swept aside, and the whole new social reform policy was adopted in America as well.

In the U.S.A. there are two great parties that have dominated politics ever since the Civil War in the 1860's, the Republicans and the Democrats. The difference between them had a definite relationship to their conceptions of government, in this case the federal government. The Democrats maintained that the individual states should have as much independent power as possible, while the Republicans wanted a strong union. This conflict had led to the Civil War itself. The Republicans also wanted to use the power of the Union to provide strong protection to native economic life, especially industry. The fact that the Democrats preferred free trade was due to their interest in exporting goods from the southern states. Yet it turned out that when the Democrats came into power, they too proceeded to expand the power of the Union and even went so far in this respect that the Republicans found it to their advantage to oppose it. As the southern states gradually came to be industrialized, the Democrats also became protectionists. In this way both parties have in reality combined to strengthen the central government.

The conditions of life in America and the extensive opportunities long existing there for economic gain and personal initiative had fostered an individualistic dogma that had become a kind of religion, a truly American outlook. This dogma was destroyed in the great economic crisis of the early 1930's. While the Republican leadership allowed the crisis to develop and expected that the old economic "laws" would straighten out distress and falling prices and unemployment by themselves, a strong demand arose among the people for active intervention on the part of the government. The state was asked to restore all that private enterprise had destroyed. It was a rebellion against the old national policy that elevated Franklin D. Roosevelt to the president's chair on a program to change these conditions, a "New Deal." In place of the free competition of previous days came a planned economy with all kinds of state interference in the economic and business life of the nation. Those who previously had been in power screamed that this was socialism and Bolshevism, un-American and in opposition to Western ideals. In many ways it *was* a kind of revolution. There were western European models for the system of social insurance that was established, including protection against unemployment and old age, as well as regulation of working hours, and other social policies. An even greater change was the policy of undertaking economic enterprises on behalf of the government— the development of water power, the conservation of natural resources, and many others. Industrial capitalism was drawn into a social cooperation it had previously opposed. It was a cultural change-over that made the state more of a basic force than ever before.

In America, however, Communists are held to be enemies of the state, and Communistic parties are legally hampered. Among European countries, the same is true in West Germany, where the Communist party is entirely banned.

It reminds one of the ban on the order of the Jesuits in the days when European countries wanted to protect themselves against the dominance of the Catholic church. In either case it is the state that wishes to maintain its power, and no other organization is allowed to resist it.

In the last few years new states have sprung into being in Asia and Africa, and have taken their places in international life. They have not reached the level of older nations of Europe and America with respect to organized social life, but in all of them the power of the state is of cardinal importance.

The two greatest of these, China and India, have very extensive traditions of culture. But the political heritage, which in a way is the basis for a national political unity, has been broken by so many historical changes that they have in reality had to build up their state on an entirely new basis. They have chosen different ways of doing it.

The new China won its freedom in war and had at least a military force to start with. It was therefore natural, perhaps, that the Chinese should choose to follow the example of Russia. They entered into a compulsory communism where economic and cultural life were subjected to the state. This is the fastest way of industrializing an old agricultural country—let the state do it.

India has much greater difficulties to face, composed as it is of many quite different nationalities. In addition, it is hampered not only by poverty and ignorance, but also by irrational compulsive ideas in its religion. It is as if a strong state power were unable to gain a foothold. The scattered little villages throughout the country often lack any kind of contact with the outer world. They have no roads, no telegraph, no telephones, so that virtually no authority can reach them. Under such circumstances the state is powerless and helpless. Yet the state, weak as it is, is their only hope for improvement and progress. India, at least, is a bit of conclusive evidence for the necessity of establishing a strong state. The Indians are trying to do so by following the example of England, the power that in its time made India into a united nation.

Chapter IX

WAR AS A DESTROYER AND A STIMULUS

"There has always been war as long as the world has existed, and there will be war in all future time as well"— so went the common saying. We who live today are easily tempted to accept this saying as truth. We have grown accustomed to expect war at practically any time.

In reality, we do not know when war began in the world. War may be defined as strife between groups. But this does not mean that strife rose immediately after groups came into being. We can not confidently speak of war until we see that people had weapons, and we get well down into history before we can be sure of it. By this time we have reached a period when states or kingdoms had come into being. Not until we have states can we truly speak of war. Some have maintained that war has its roots in the natural aggressiveness of all men. However, when people have united into states, purely personal aggression comes to have less and less significance. Broadly speaking, we can probably say that war is initiated either for the sake of power or for booty, and in simple conditions of life these motives may be clear enough. The more developed and complex the social structure becomes, the more the reasons for war are hidden, as the state grows more impersonal. For this reason it is quite conceivable that war may cease, although the individual human being still retains his aggressiveness. The social institutions may be able to restrain his warlike aggression.

This is not the topic of our chapter, however. I wish to speak about the past, when there were certainly more than enough wars. Old textbooks of history contained practically nothing but war. In the present day, many have reacted against this practice and have demanded the exclusion of war from the books. It is true that little is lost if we no longer ask the pupils to memorize all the battles of ancient wars, such as those of the Punic Wars, or the Thirty Years' War, the Wars of Louis XIV, or Frederick the Great—Höchstädt 1703, Blenheim 1704, Ramillies 1707, Oudenarde 1708, Malplaquet 1709, etc. etc. There is not much history to be learned from these.

On the other hand, no one can deny that wars have left deep traces on the historical development of most nations. It is of the greatest interest to explore and explain why wars have been waged and what these wars have produced.[45]

We have already seen that most states were founded by force, born in blood just like man himself. Since their foundation, states have built their existence and their policy on the concept of *power*. The Italian political thinker Machiavelli was the one who developed this concept of power into a political principle. The Machiavellian principle declared that anything which benefited the state was right—might was right. This reasoning is still alive in our own day. I remember that my history teacher in high school said as a matter of course that ordinary personal morality did not apply to states. They had a morality of their own that involved power and gain. Not until the nineteenth century did some people begin to believe and demand that even in foreign relations the great moral principles should be applied. In practice there has been little of this.

The defense of war has always been that states needed this instrument to promote their interests. These were generally called "vital interests." The most profound effect of war may be psychological—that war has taught people to think of power as the foremost problem in international politics. It is "naive" to reckon with moral motives. I will not judge this mode of thinking—we meet it every day in the press, in political speeches, and in diplomatic notes. It is the spiritual climate in which we live.

Of course war can benefit not only those who win, but even those who lose. When the Roman Empire was founded in the West and the Chinese Empire in the East, peace was thereby established throughout huge areas. People who lived in these empires could boast of this peace after they had forgotten their old independence. The other side of this picture is that just as war could build great empires, so it could also destroy them. This is what happened to both of these empires. In war such states were not only split up, but large parts of them were harried year after year until poverty replaced their former wealth, and their population went into a decline. This is what occurred when barbarians, whether Germanic or Tartar, streamed across their borders bringing murder and havoc.

In most cases war has established the borders between states. When a state then expands its territory, it usually does so at the expense of another state. If the balance of power shifts, the other state can recover what it has lost, so that one province can pass back and forth from one master to another, as, for instance, Alsace-Lorraine. In such cases contemporaries and successors may feel sympathy for one side or the other, but history has generally been sympathetic to whichever state had the highest culture, in case there was any difference between them in this respect.

War has had the effect of displacing cultural borders as well as political ones. After the Romans had conquered Gaul, they made it into a land of culture. When Franks, Burgundians, and Visigoths later overwhelmed the country, they had to build on Roman culture. The Arabs made themselves masters in many Mediterranean countries, and they were able to show the world a brilliant cultural development in Spain and Sicily. In both places they acquired the old culture of these countries and added to it in certain ways. But in all of North Africa they destroyed the Greco-Roman culture that had grown up there, and they substituted no new culture in its place. Christianity was also introduced by force in many countries. There can be no doubt that the Spaniards in America combined their introduction of Christianity with the destruction of a great deal of old culture, a destruction so thorough that even the testimonials of this culture were largely destroyed. In this way gain and loss can be chalked up for the same historical event.

Religious wars have often been fiercer among sects within the same religion than among people of quite different religions. Surely no European war was ever fought more bitterly than the one in which Catholic and Protestant Christians opposed one another. In many countries this was a civil war. Countrymen who fight each other hate each other the more because their opponents are felt to be traitors to that which should be sacred for them all. When Germany became the battlefield of the Thirty Years' War, the country was ravaged so frightfully that it took a long time before it could be restored to its former prosperity and population growth. German culture was also weakened, perhaps by the vulgarization of thinking during the protracted warfare. The war was to a great extent carried on by professional mercenaries who respected neither material nor spiritual values.

Neither side won a clear-cut victory for its religion. This was no doubt best for religion, since the hostile sects were forced to endure one another in an armed state of coexistence. The war itself had been a struggle for political rather than religious supremacy, and the nation that issued from the war as the strongest power was Catholic France, which had allied itself with the Protestants. This war gave France its position of leadership in Europe for the next two centuries.

In the same period colonial policy also drew the European states into new wars. These might even be called world wars because they were fought on all the oceans and in the continents of America, Asia, and Africa, besides Europe. The most important causes of these wars were economic, and the result of them was that England gained the supremacy of the seas.

Another result of the struggles between the great powers of Europe was the growth of a policy of neutrality. Smaller states felt themselves threatened by these conflicts, and they sought protection in neutrality. They could no longer have any hope of carrying on war, and therefore made peace into a world program. One may say that this made a virtue of necessity, but it was still a virtue—a desire to reduce the area of armed conflict.

The great powers might have reasons of their own for hesitating to wage war. For one thing, great numbers of their own people were more and more opposed to war. This shows us clearly enough that personal aggressiveness was no longer an important motivation of war. Indeed war became a hindrance to the general interests of commerce, and an interference in all kinds of cultural development. Toward the end of the nineteenth century it came to be generally believed that culture, at least in western Europe and North America, had reached a point that made war virtually unthinkable.

In the 1890's a Russian financier, Johann von Bloch, maintained that the technique of armaments had reached a point that would make any war completely self-destructive for all participants, and that therefore no government would dare to unleash it. In 1910 the English economist Norman Angell published a book called *The Great Illusion*, in which he pointed out that the victors in a war would be economically destroyed to just as great an extent as the losers, so that it would be sheer madness for any government to start a war.

Nevertheless we know that new wars did come, vast world wars, one worse than the other. The power struggle among the great nations set aside all the rational arguments against war.

The craving for power has been a motivation of war from the oldest times to the present. But we find some wars that have been fought not only for power, but also against it. These are the wars of rebellion when peoples have risen against oppression. We generally consider such wars as a forward cultural step. This is because freedom seems to us to be a positive goal, a human right, and a people fighting for its freedom is looked on with sympathy by all who accept this principle.

Not all revolutions, however, have freedom as their goal. The revolt in Spain led by Franco in 1936 was directed against a liberal and democratic government, and it succeeded with the help of dictator governments in other countries. The free countries of the world were lukewarm in their sympathy and gave little or no help to the defense of Spanish freedom.

Revolts for freedom have many a time shaken the world and initiated even more strife. I believe the first revolt of this kind that had its aftereffects in other countries was the uprising of the Hussites in Bohemia in the 1420's and 1430's. This spread to Germany and caused unrest in the Baltic countries, including Sweden. The church leaders in all Catholic countries were terrified by it, and the Pope preached a crusade against it. It was suppressed by force of arms, for the Hussites had been premature in their demands for religious and social freedom.

In modern times such revolts have been more successful. In the 1820's, when the Greeks made their revolution against Turkish domination, it was comparatively easy for them to win general sympathy. They were revolting against "the infidels," and, besides, the entire civilized world treasured the memories of Thermopylae and Salamis. Philhellenism was a rallying cry for lovers of freedom in the period of reaction then dominant in Europe. Nevertheless it was probably the struggle for power that led England and Russia to give the rebels military assistance. Without such assistance Greece could not at that time have won her freedom.

All the other revolts in the Europe of that day were struck down by force. The Greek revolt became a harbinger of the spirit of freedom in Europe. The example was reinforced by contemporary revolts in South and Central America.

These are examples of the way in which war could promote progress, though we must add that it was the suppression of freedom under tyrannical power that made it necessary to carry on wars of freedom.

War has spurred uprisings and even revolutions in certain cases, not because the war had this as its goal, but because it brought with it such distress and dissatisfaction that the people were stimulated to revolt against their government or to demand reforms in social and political organization.

Russia here affords us some good examples. Whenever the government was defeated in war, it was compelled to yield to popular demands that it had previously rejected. The demands grew stronger among the people as the government was weakened. The Crimean War led to the freeing of Russian slaves in 1856. The calamitous war with Japan compelled the czar to grant certain rights of self-rule in Russia and Finland in 1905. The World War ten years later brought with it two revolutions, first a liberal one in the spring of 1917, and then the Bolshevik one in the fall. The defeat of the government became a victory for movements among the people. Finland and the other Baltic states gained their independence on the same occasion.

The same World War led to revolution and a republic in Germany in 1918. I well remember the jubilation among lovers of freedom throughout the world when daily telegrams brought the news of royal houses that had had to give up their power for the benefit of the people. These were fruits of the war that all could hail. On the other hand, we were constantly reminded of the distress the same war had caused in Germany.

The effects of war were not limited to those who took part in them, but spread to other countries as well. Some countries even profited from the wars of others, or rather, the merchants in such neutral countries profited. We know this well from World War I in Norway, when wealth poured down on some circles, while others had perhaps poorer circumstances than before. Such a development tended to sharpen inner conflicts and to stimulate new demands on the government for state interference and social reform. When the world became as totalitarian as it did in the Second World War, so that all talents and capacities of society were enlisted in the service of the war, there was little opportunity for gain on the part of individuals. Nevertheless, the distress of the whole world led to new appeals to the state for its assistance.

Every state has always had to face the possibility of war and be prepared for it. This has laid great burdens on their peoples through taxes and military service. It has seriously affected the economy not only of the state but also of its private citizens. The resulting competition of armaments has added another cause of war. Alliances and other preventive actions have been universal instruments of international politics. In this way war has conspicuous consequences even when there is no war.

It has often been said that people benefit from an occasional war. The argument has been that war requires certain virtues or traits of character that otherwise tend to be dormant, such as patriotic feeling, the spirit of sacrifice, mutual helpfulness, and heroic courage. It is true that war calls for these virtues, though society certainly needs them and calls upon them in times of peace as well. It is also true that war compels all to apply their talents with even greater vigor than they do in daily life. This is not in itself any reason to wish for war. There is an old saying to the effect that necessity is the mother of invention, but we do not therefore conclude that necessity should be encouraged.

No one can deny that war has stimulated many inventions that later have become useful in daily life. When firearms were invented and employed in the wars of the fourteenth century, this was followed by their use for hunting. Guns were more effective than traps and snares and less painful to the animals. War can call forth new techniques of benefit to men in other fields than armaments. In World War I there was a fat shortage in many countries. In England and Norway scientists were called on for an invention that would make whale fat usable as human food. The task was solved in both countries, and they were thereby protected from a lack of fats. In all the wars of modern times much effort has gone into the discovery of good remedies for disease and wounds, and these have assisted medical science in peacetime as well. Airplanes for transporting people and goods through the air were invented a few years before World War I, but the need of using them in the war produced the greatest advances in the building of planes.

During World War II much effort was expended on solving the problem of splitting the atom. It would hardly have been possible to solve it so quickly if the goal had not been one of making bombs for use in the war. The experiments were so tremendously expensive that one could not expect them to be undertaken under normal conditions. After the war this work continued even more intensely because the fear of war was still very much alive. We already have evidence that this invention can become a servant of peaceful goals as well.

The judgment of history is likely to be that these advances would have been made even without war, though hardly as soon. The old saying holds for war, too, that nothing is so bad that there is nothing good in it. The best one can say about war is that whatever it has given us of good has usually resulted from an effort to combat its evil results.

In any case it is clear that war has been a tremendous factor in human life. Whether as a destroyer or a stimulus, it has attained such power that we hardly dare look its effects squarely in the eye. If the world is to continue to exist, it will be necessary to prevent all war in the future.

Chapter X

SCIENCE AS A
FORCE IN SOCIETY

The importance of science in the life of society has been deeply imprinted on all of us who are living today. We have observed how the science of steam and electricity has been transforming society for a century and a half. Within my own lifetime I have seen the coming of the telephone and the electric light, the discovery of microbes and vitamins, the building of chemical factories, the invention of the phonograph and the cinema, of automobiles and motorboats, of airplanes and submarines. Every day we hear of new machines and remarkable discoveries science has produced for us. We are told of how the scientists are working on all the novelties, both promising and terrifying, that we can expect as a result of the splitting of the "unsplittable" atom.

Although we have given these sciences such names as physics, chemistry, or biology, they only continue an effort that man has been engaged in as long as he has lived on earth—the effort to become acquainted with the forces of nature and to harness them to his use. This was actually one of the important ways of building human society.

Natural science has been a part of history from the very beginning.

We make a distinction between natural sciences and humanistic sciences. In the Middle Ages a new Greek word, "metaphysics," was created for the science of everything beyond the physical. Much of this turned out to be purely speculative thinking about universal laws, abstracts, removed from everything physical. Little by little, however, we learned that all humanistic science actually was intimately connected with natural science. Even a discipline so apparently abstract as mathematics led directly into natural science. What would physics and chemistry have been today without mathematical thinking? Men like Gibbs and Einstein made possible the greatest of the inventions. In the final analysis all science is intellectual effort. For this reason the human intellect is itself the greatest force in historical progress.

Those sciences that we consider to be particularly humanistic are also compelled to work with actual conditions of human life if they are to make any progress. This is true of economics, linguistics, psychology, history, theology, and even philosophy. Each of these sciences, in turn, is a part of social life and a force in the building of society. It is a task of historical research to trace the social effects of all scientific work. History throws light on the continuity between past and present, and in so doing helps us to understand the forces of life. In this way history itself becomes a force in our lives.

We often speak of our "historical heritage." There is no doubt that the highest culture of our day has a heritage that goes back not only to the classical period of Europe, but also to the thinking of Egypt, Babylonia, Palestine, even India and China. Our knowledge of this continuity strengthens the forces of culture and the hope for progress of the generations now living. We would cut off our own roots if we forgot this connection.

Theology is perhaps the discipline that gives us the strongest sense of the power of the past. Theology works with the study and interpretation of writings that are two thousand or more years old, and it compels every new generation to make up its mind about these writings. The Ten Commandments, which Christians and Jews alike regard as the framework of our morality, may be close to three thousand years old. In the same way the scholars of China, India, and the Mohammedan countries work with ancient religious and philosophical writings that still constitute the textbooks and the moral codes of each new generation.

We know that the Jewish-Christian Bible has absorbed a great deal from Babylonian thinking into its Old Testament. We know that the New Testament, especially the Gospel of St. John and the Letters of Paul, has learned a great deal from Greek philosophy, which therefore is actively with us to this very day. When the famous church father Augustine at the beginning of the Middle Ages shaped his great survey of fate and law, he too had Greek philosophy behind him. His work became the basis and the inspiration of Protestant as well as Catholic theology and doctrine. At the same time Roman law became the model of legal practice in one medieval kingdom after the other. Cultural as well as legal activity in the European Middle Ages built in important ways on the heritage from Greece and Rome.

When the Christian philosophers of the Middle Ages tried to construct a universal view of life, they found their starting point in Plato and Aristotle. The burning question for them was the conflict between physical reality and abstract generalization. In their scholastic disputes they set up a series of alternatives which could be answered either yes or no—*sic et non*, as a textbook by Abelard was actually called. This was a training in thinking which found its fruition in great philosophical systems, above all that of Thomas Aquinas.

Even though such philosophical speculations were limited to the theologians of the church, the universities sent out preachers who had learned to think at these institutions and who became the leaders of the common people. After this came another and more worldly movement, the Renaissance, which was a rebirth of the ancient culture. This movement was social, cultural, and scientific, and it was strongly suffused with Greek learning. Political thinkers began to discuss problems of political structure on the basis of Greek models, and they used Greek terms and definitions for such phenomena as democracy and aristocracy, oligarchy and monarchy. The theologians were given an opportunity now to study the writings of the New Testament in their oldest, Greek form, and the philosophers had the privilege of reading Greek works in the original language. It was a revival of ancient heritage that brought a fresh life with it. Philological and historical science made the connection with the past more consciously alive in wider circles than ever before.

In the next centuries this new knowledge was not lost but strengthened. When we reach the great revolutions of the eighteenth century, we find a spirit of liberty that was modeled on the writings of Greeks and Romans. This could take purely external forms, such as the adoption of heroic Greek and Latin names, or the making of clothes on classical models, or the erection of buildings imitated from the Capitoline Hill and the Acropolis. When they strove for freedom and sacrificed themselves for the fatherland, they felt akin to the Greeks and the Romans. Here was an example that could inspire. American Revolutionary generals corresponded about subjects from Greco-Roman history and literature.

We have mentioned already in another connection the impulse given by the Renaissance for each nation to explore its own past. We see how learned men in Germany could take Arminius, a leader in the conflict with the Roman Empire, and turn him into a national hero by rebaptizing him with the German name Herrmann. Other memories of the past were employed also to strengthen the German spirit of independence. Even the French, who had a very strong Latin heritage, sometimes fell back on native models. In Normandy, for example, they built churches in old Romanesque style instead of the classical Renaissance style when they wanted to break with the "barbaric" Gothic. The French hero of freedom was a Gaulish rebel, King Vercingetorix. In our own country of Norway a whole school of learned men arose in the sixteenth century who cultivated the ancient sagas while they dreamed that Norway might again rise to greatness. The most striking movement of this kind is perhaps the learned Swedish Renaissance, which bent all efforts to the creation of a great national past. The founder of Swedish historiography, Olaus Magnus, published a great work in 1555 on the history of the Nordic peoples. The purpose was to demonstrate the accomplishments of the Swedes in ancient times—their courage, their law-abiding qualities, their virtue and honor. He included Goths and Lombards, and even the Scythian peoples among their ancestors. He used old Danish chronicles to prove that the Swedes had been better than the Danes. He made old Norwegian heroes into Swedes. He constructed a long Swedish royal genealogy in a period without historical sources. The purpose of it all was to prove that the Swedes had once been the greatest people on earth, and therefore ought to be able to win back this position once more.

This movement was a general European one. It had as its function the awakening of national feelings among the people and filling them with the spirit of history.[46] This movement was strengthened during the following centuries. I do not for a moment maintain that it was learning, or the agitation of learned men, that called forth national sentiment. Other and stronger forces did that, but there can be no doubt that research into the past and historical writing gave color and strength to the national feeling.

We are well informed on the importance of the old Norwegian royal sagas in the national liberation of Norway, particularly in the year 1814. Jacob Aall exaggerated somewhat when he wrote that the sixteenth-century translation by Peder Claussøn of Snorri's *History*, which was republished in 1751, circulated "among the leading peasants and constituted their favorite reading."[47] However, reminiscences of this book were certainly alive among the men of Eidsvoll. Much of their learning came from a work published in 1789 by the Danish scholar Tyge Rothe and entitled *Nordens Statsforfatning* ("The Political Constitution of Scandinavia"). On the basis of Norwegian sources this work described the earliest period as having had a vigorous peasant democracy. It was a period of "udal rights with freedom of the people." This was the ideal they wanted to restore in 1814, and explains their emphasis on the udal (*odel*) rights, the voting privileges of the landowning peasants, and the name *Odelsting* for the lower house of the Norwegian parliament. Snorri did become popular reading when he was translated in 1838–1839 by Jacob Aall. His work sold nearly four thousand copies.

Norwegian national feeling was further strengthened by the writings of the "Norwegian school of history," particularly in the 1850's by the great *History of the Norwegian People* by P. A. Munch. Munch and his colleague Rudolf Keyser led a vigorous campaign to reclaim the Old Norse poetry and sagas for Norway. They even had a special doctrine about the early immigration to Scandinavia that separated Norwegians from Danes and Swedes in their very origins. It was crucial for them that Norwegians should liberate themselves from the "Danish period," culturally as well as politically.

Historical writing in the same nationalistic vein was characteristic of a number of other European countries. The closest counterpart to the Norwegian historical school was the lifework of the Bohemian writer Palacky. He too wished to prove the historical right to independence of his people, the Czechs. The national idea was vital enough also among historians in Germany, France, and England, as well as in those nations that were still struggling for their independence.

In 1918 I wrote a paper, "Historiography and National Growth,"[48] in which I demonstrated that the problem of national independence for Norway expressed itself as a conflict between two views of history. In the 1860's there was a great discussion concerning the question, "Who are our true ancestors?" The choice lay between those who had ruled and organized the country in the Danish period, and those who obscurely and almost in secret had maintained the traditions of an older period right through the Danish rule. Learned scholars like Michael Birkeland and T. H. Aschehoug favored the former, while an equally learned scholar like J. E. Sars favored the latter. In this conflict past and future were so intimately intertwined that it was not easy to say whether one's view of the past determined one's thoughts of the future, or if it was the other way around. Purely psychologically we tend to feel that the arguments follow the point of view. Even so, the arguments do have a certain force. History became a powerful weapon in winning over the people to one or another policy in the questions of independence vs. Scandinavianism in politics and language. In opposition to the English saying, "History is past politics," I could maintain that the discussion in Norway clearly showed that history very well can be present politics.

Other topics treated in that paper included the interpretation of documents concerning the constitutional position of Norway in the Danish period and the organization of the union between Norway and Sweden in 1814. Historians and jurists in the nineteenth century interpreted these documents according to the political views of their own times. These are instructive testimonials to the intimate connection between historical thinking and contemporary life, and show how history could be more or less deliberately used in the controversies of the day.

In this connection, however, it would be more profitable to say something about the way in which historical and literary research in the 1870's assisted the realistic movement in cultural and literary life, which won its victory at this time. Earlier scholars had believed that the Old Norse poems in the *Elder Edda* were the product of an old Nordic "folk spirit." The Danish heretic Edwin Jessen, and after him J. E. Sars and Sophus Bugge in Norway, showed that this poetry had its origin in particular circumstances of the Viking period, including strong influences from other countries. This put an end to a great deal of romantic thinking, in Denmark as in Norway.

The historical views of Sars were victorious both in domestic politics and in the conflict with Sweden. Later, at the turn of the twentieth century, social and economic questions came to the fore, which furnished new points of view for historical research. The national movement now loomed against a background of social conflict and could be reinterpreted as the entry of one social class after another into the life of the nation. Nobleman, citizen, peasant, and farmer, each one separately uniting with his fellows, rose forth to demand his rightful position and eventually created a general solidarity of society. This new historical outlook was also influential in helping solve the question of the Norwegian language, the other national problem that had entered into the controversy between Sars, on the one hand, and Birkeland and Aschehoug, on the other. Here, too, the emphasis was shifted from a purely nationalistic idea to one of social unification. The labor movement and the language movement were hereby given a new historical background, shedding new light on their own struggle.

It has been natural for me as a historian to trace first the influence of historical science on the thinking of an age. I am, of course, clearly aware that other sciences have had the same kind of influence, and in some situations a much greater influence. My references earlier to the revolutionary effects of natural science in modern times were only for the purpose of reminding us of the obvious. Everyone is clearly aware of the power of science. Its effect is not, however, entirely on external things like communication, productivity, etc. Natural science can reshape the thinking of humanity just as well as can history. Science has had a particularly great effect in the important area of religion.

The Greek philosophers had shaped a new view of the world that liberated their thinking from many religious bonds. These ideas did not reach wider circles until modern times. Only when the Polish astronomer Copernicus demonstrated that the earth was a planet that orbits around the sun did people gradually begin to realize that the earth and its inhabitants were not the center of the universe. The Pope even condemned his teaching as contrary to Holy Scripture. Then the circumnavigations of the earth made it obvious to everyone that the earth was indeed shaped like a ball and not like a pancake. Giordano Bruno was the first to point out the philosophical consequences of the new cosmogony when he deposed a personal God. For this heresy he paid with his life. Then the discoveries of Kepler, Galileo, and Newton brought natural law into the whole system for good. Voltaire could even mock the imperfections of God's creation and ridicule the arrogance of men who believed that a God would direct all things in life on behalf of such miserable little creatures.

It became impossible to maintain the belief that everything in the Bible was God's word and, literally, God's truth. This became even more evident when the geologists began to explore the origin of the earth. After that came the higher criticism of the Bible, which grew to be a science built up of philology and history. Individual research took the place of blind faith in authority. This was a tremendous intellectual revolution, and it swept everything before it.

The great clash between faith and science came in the 1870's after Darwin had published his work *The Descent of Man*. Here he gave concrete form to the doctrine of evolution that various scientists before him had proposed. Man and monkey had previously been regarded as two distinct levels in the zoological world, but for Darwin their similarity was evidence of kinship in such a way that the higher level had developed from the lower one. This was in direct opposition to the biblical doctrine of man's creation, and many people were outraged at the idea that man was descended from monkeys. This particular point in his theory and others were altered as a result of later research, but the basic concept of a gradual progress up to the final human being has remained. This was the heart of the conflict, and the success of the evolutionary concept was one of the greatest revolutions in the history of human thought.

Henceforth the laws of nature were established as masters of man in a much more direct way than ever before. This was perhaps the strongest factor in the realism that now became dominant in literature. From it was born a scientific determinism quite different from the fatalism under God which had been proclaimed before this time. Man learned to feel himself "under the law" in quite a different way from before. The question of the relationship between freedom and law became a part of history also and was discussed for all aspects of human life. The question is still awaiting its final solution. The main thing is that our discussion of the problem has been put on a new footing through the emergence of natural science.

The application of science to man himself led to the birth of a new science, namely, psychology. Up to this time psychology had been little more than speculation. Now it grew into a discipline that even could employ experimental methods. Another link was thereby forged between animals and men, and no one was now offended by this conception. Man had learned to look on himself as the highest member —but still a member—of the vast animal world. In this way science has transformed us all.

Chapter XI

INFLUENCE AMONG NATIONS

The historian who is concerned with a single people or state inevitably tends to look for the continuity of its history in internal circumstances and national growth. It is the same as with the individual: one should first try to understand his life as an expression of his own personal qualities and abilities.

However, everyone learns from others, and so do nations and societies. We do not understand them fully unless we consider what they have learned from others.

It can often be quite unconscious, as we know it is with children. They absorb from their environment an endless array of impressions that help to shape them into adults. Sigrid Undset once commented on the alleged miracle attributed to St. Catherine of Siena, according to which she knew in detail the lives of many holy persons about whom she had never received any instruction. Although Sigrid Undset was a devout Catholic, the psychologist in her led her to remark, drily, "A child of six can absorb a tremendous amount of knowledge without knowing where it comes from." It is the same with groups of people as well.

They can blot up, as it were, from the atmosphere around them a great many ideas that they have never read or been formally taught. Ideas can infect just as well as invisible bacteria. Cultural influences range from country to country without anyone's knowing how they travel. These influences are tremendously significant in the development of a people. Isolated peoples can easily stand still through hundreds and thousands of years. The impulse to progress nearly always comes from the outside.

The only reservation one can make concerning the strength of such influences is that certain conditions must be fulfilled if a people is going to accept them. The thinking or the skills of one people may be on so high a level that other peoples do not have the capacity to acquire them or exploit them. This is generally a question of time, just as it is within a given people—there, too, ideas or inventions may often have to wait for a long time before they are generally accepted. We may then say that a process of maturation is necessary. But is there any people that cannot mature, that does not have the capacity for learning new things? One can hear assertions to this effect, but history offers no evidence to support them.

Learning and influence have been going on around the world through all ages as far back as we can go. This is true of material as well as spiritual values. Archaeology reports it from the very earliest Stone Age. Some things may, of course, have been invented independently in various places. But people have had to learn most of their crafts and arts from others. Such things as boring shaft holes in a stone ax, or making fish hooks, or firing pottery—is it conceivable that such inventions can have been made independently by the people of each country? The fact that we in Norway can find stone artifacts made in Denmark, or that pottery from southern Norway can be found in the northernmost parts of the country, shows beyond a doubt how objects could travel very far, even in ages when travel must have been very difficult.

The closer we get to our own time, and the more elaborate the techniques, the more necessary it has become for people to be taught. Extracting copper and iron, silver and gold, has never been an accomplishment that everyone could master, and even less the forging and molding of the metals into their final shape. Wherever it has not been possible to import such products from abroad, it has become necessary to learn the art of making them. The word "copper" quite simply means "from Cyprus." We know that iron was first extracted in Asia Minor, and that the word "iron" in Germanic is a loanword from Celtic. Archaeologists can follow the spread of patterns of decoration from country to country. Even religious beliefs and customs have been passed on from one country to another.

Man's first domesticated animal was the dog. Dogs may have come from various places, descended from jackals in the south and from wolves in the north. Other domestic animals were adopted after the example of neighbors in ever-widening circles.

When people changed over to agriculture, they had to learn from others about grains as well as implements. There is actually an elaborate world history already in the prehistoric period. This has continued ever since without cessation.

In those matters that affect our physical existence we all know this very well from our daily life. Aside from the raw materials that we eat and drink, there is hardly a single thing we use that does not have foreign origin in one way or another. I need say no more about this, but will turn to some questions of cultural influence, the kind of thing that is generally called "currents of culture." We use this term so easily and consider it to be a matter of course that cultural life should spread from one country to another. Yet such movements may often be very complex and are not always easy to explain.

The first great cultural movements that we know were spread far and wide in the world were the three great religions—Buddhism, Christianity, and Mohammedanism. Much thought has been applied to the question of precisely why these three religions should have won so much power. One can hardly say that the question has been fully clarified. It does not help to say that each of these religions gave to the men of its area something that was richer and better than they knew before.

We shall consider Christianity, simply because I know the history of this religion best. In the later period, after Christianity had become a state religion in the powerful Roman Empire, one can certainly say it was introduced in a number of countries by pure force. Even in this case, however, we must reckon with a psychological change, a revolution of the inmost emotional life of the converts before they could truly be called Christian. In the period before the government backed it, the influences that created the Christian movement were purely religious.

Within the borders of the Roman Empire there was a great deal of what can be called religious restlessness at the time when Christianity appeared. There were many who were not content with the classical Greek and Roman religions. We can take it for granted that there was a trend toward monotheism, both in intellectual circles and among the common people: most persons put their trust in only one of the gods. All of them believed in a life after death. They yearned, however, for a more intimate association with the divine power. A whole procession of Oriental religions came to them from Western Asia and Egypt with mystical messages and sacrifices that appealed to this religious need. They found many followers in the Western world, and we see traces of them all the way from Rome itself to the outermost provinces along the border.

The characteristic feature of Christianity was that more than any of the others it appealed to the individual conscience. Socrates had spoken of the hidden voice in the heart that guided the individual to what was right. This might be sufficient for intellectuals, but Christianity went farther because it wished to awaken men to an awareness of their own sinfulness and implant in them a need for salvation from the punishment for their sins. We have in the Scandinavian languages an interesting linguistic trace of the difference between pagan and Christian thinking. The Old Norsemen believed that the dead would go to the kingdom of Hel, the goddess of death. The Christians added to her name the word *viti*, that is, punishment, so that the pagan kingdom of the dead turned into a frightening hell (*helviti*). This idea did not greatly appeal to the most educated, but it found ready response among the common people. Christianity had a social mission besides its religious one. It was aimed at the little man in society and wanted to give the commoners new confidence by assuring them that they were all children of God. The love of God the Father would save them. In this way Christianity fulfilled a human need. This must have been the most important condition for its rapid spread in the Roman Empire.

As far as its success among the Germanic barbarians was concerned, the problem may be a little different. This has been most carefully studied for Norway, because we know more about the pagan beliefs of the old Norwegians than of the other Germanic peoples. Attempts have been made to analyze the features in Norse paganism that could most easily lead into Christianity. It must be confessed that we know more about the mythology than we do about the religious faith of the Norse pagans. But here too it appears that most people put their trust in just one god. Even if they knew about other gods, they found it easy to transfer this mode of thinking to the Christian Trinity, not to speak of all the saints which came in with Christianity. All kinds of magic could easily pass from one religion to the other. The confession of sins was perhaps the most difficult point for these people. The fear of hell was accepted much sooner. However, it does appear that a much greater transformation of religious feeling was necessary here than among the people of the Roman Empire. Southern Europe required a couple of hundred years before Christianity won its foothold. It would no doubt have taken equally long in Norway if the state had not applied its mailed fist.

These historical developments show us that certain particular conditions need to be present before a cultural movement can gain a foothold in new countries. Those who are going to accept and assimilate learning and influence from abroad need to have a kind of spiritual kinship with their teachers and also be in a situation that gives them easy access to the new ideas.

It took a long time before any other movement arose with the power and breadth of Christianity. One of the circumstances that conditioned its wide spread from the remote corner of the world where it began was the peace and the ease of communication established by the Roman Empire. The Apostle Paul had a great advantage in the fact that he was a Roman citizen. After the breakup of this world empire, the world was noisy with war. The unity between Asia and Africa on the one hand and Europe on the other was broken by the Mohammedan advance, especially when the Turks made their victorious campaigns. There is something of an illusion in the old assertion that the Crusades introduced new contacts and new cultural influences between East and West. War rarely does much to promote friendship and cooperation. The Mohammedan influences that were accepted in Europe came for the most part from the Arabic centers of culture in Sicily and Spain. There the Europeans could learn about Arabian art and natural science. The Arabs could become transmitters to Europe of the Indian system of numbers and the Chinese printing of books, just as they also revived their knowledge of Greek thought. But there was no longer a united world of culture.

Within the Western world of Christianity there was a common cultural life. This was maintained by the Catholic (i.e., "universal") church, which in all countries paid allegiance to the Pope in Rome and had Latin as its language of culture. The art of the church, from architecture to music, followed the same patterns everywhere. The language that united the educated and book-learned classes helped to separate them from the people, so that folk culture was for the most part limited to the area of each nation. Even so it did happen that popular uprisings spread from country to country. This was especially true of heretical movements directed against the papacy. The rebellion of the Hussites re-echoed throughout Europe, even up to Scandinavia. The period of the Reformation stirred up a spiritual conflict that involved all the peoples of western Europe. This can be attributed to the strengthened commercial contacts and to the new middle-class culture that was growing up alongside the old ecclesiastical culture. A new Europe was emerging.

Latin was gradually given up in favor of the national languages, not only for poetry, but for all kinds of science as well. Nevertheless, European cultural cooperation was stronger than before because greater segments of the people got a chance to participate in it.

The eighteenth century was the great era of the new European culture. A campaign for intellectual liberation was launched, above all by the French men of letters, who were the leading agitators for freedom. Voltaire, Montesquieu, and Rousseau were read and discussed in every country and stirred up controversy in many places. A revolution was in the making, which was to bring with it great changes in the state and in society.

The first political revolution was the American uprising against English colonial policy. The result was the emergence of the United States as a force in world history. In my book *The American Spirit in Europe* I discussed the economic and cultural influences of America on Europe.[49] I pointed out that the first man from America who made a place for himself in European thinking was Benjamin Franklin. He was a genuine representative of the middle class that now was taking over the leadership in all work for progress. He was the natural spokesman for the program that had been formulated by the Italian jurist Beccaria: the greatest happiness of the greatest number. He inculcated the utilitarian bourgeois philosophy by short and amusing sayings, which made it easy to accept. Franklin was a welcome guest in all circles. Besides this, he was the one who, like a second Prometheus, had brought lightning down from heaven with his lightning rod!

He became the first spokesman for the American Revolution, and made even this amusing by his speeches in the British parliament. The Revolution itself was serious enough, and it made a tremendous impression round about in Europe. There was something bourgeois in this Revolution, too, since it was a struggle on behalf of the freedom of merchants, including even the freedom to smuggle and carry on piracy. But the very fact that it turned into a war elevated it to a higher plane. The Revolution won a philosophical setting when Thomas Jefferson associated it with the French concept of universal human rights. European idealists took service in the Revolutionary army. Afterwards they carried American ideas of freedom back home again. These ideas had originally come to America from England, but now they were turned against England herself. Even Europeans who were friendly to England rejoiced at the American success. There were leaders of English liberal politics, like the elder and younger William Pitt, who took the side of the American colonists. George Washington became a popular hero in all countries that longed for freedom. He was the first freedom hero of modern times.

The victory of the American Revolution was the first serious blow to the economic system of mercantilism. This accorded well with the first great scientific blow directed at the system, which was made by the Scotchman Adam Smith in the same year as America proclaimed its freedom. The victory heartened all European friends of freedom. It seemed, said the young Goethe, as if a yoke had been removed from all the nations of Europe. The Americans had turned into a reality all the theory that so far had lived only in books. There is a direct line from the American Revolution to the great French Revolution. There human rights were proclaimed as a universal program for the whole world, and Jefferson actually collaborated with the French republicans. The system of government that came out of the American war for freedom was one of the models for the constitution of free Norway in 1814 and also for the free Belgian constitution of 1831.

Before long the American Revolution was overshadowed

by the French, which became an explosive force throughout Europe, and even farther away, above all in South America.

In the nineteenth century one could finally begin speaking of a true world culture. Movements in art and literature began to run parallel in every country. The same political ideals became a subject of controversy among all peoples. Science and technology no longer knew any national borders.

Here I must again return to America. Before the century ended, people were beginning to talk about the danger of Europe's and even the world's becoming "Americanized." Over there, in the new society, it was much easier for new ideas to win favor because they met less resistance than in the old world. The triumph of democracy came first in America, and established a model for the world. The Frenchman de Tocqueville's book about American democracy (1835–1840) became a kind of bible for European democrats. America was thought of as the "free country" above all others, a kind of ideal country where people longed to go.

But most "American" of all was the dominance of technology in society. England, with her machines for spinning and weaving, had originated the Industrial Revolution in the eighteenth century and had later revolutionized communications by the invention of the steam engine. But the leadership in technical invention eventually passed over to America.

It began with the triumph of American agricultural machines at the London World Exposition in 1851. These had a tremendous influence in changing the methods of work and production in agricultural societies. At the same time came the sewing machine, which even affected life within the four walls of the home. Invention after invention followed, with revolutionary effects on industry, communications, and art. I do not need to point this out in detail. I must, however, mention one particular feature that applied to everything made by machinery. This was the principle of standardization, namely, that each particular part of an instrument shall be made exactly alike so that it can be replaced by another part of the same kind. Standardization penetrated more and more deeply into daily life. Everything that people were going to use, whether for furniture or clothing, was made alike for everybody's use, without regard for individual taste or desire. This could make life easier and cheaper and was therefore "democratic." It helped to create better conditions of life for the lower classes, and thereby it lifted them up on the social scale. But was there not at the same time something that was lost? This was the kind of "Americanism" that other people began to fear.

I well remember the first time I went to America. It was in the beginning of October 1908, and there was a tremendous heat wave in New York. I put on a straw hat, which at that time was usually worn in the summer heat. This I should not have done, for it was not customary to do so after October 1st. People actually threatened to knock that hat off my head. This was an expression of the standardization that was a part of the new machine society. Such standardization could extend to other areas as well, even to the life of the mind. This was a danger that gave many people cause to worry, and they resisted the "Americanization" that in this way was threatening Europe.

In America itself standardization has been developed so far that it has been able to support many kinds of taste and thereby give an opportunity for individualization. As an example, one might think of the great variety of shoes that are made in factories today. Americans have themselves been leaders in this kind of de-Americanization and thereby given the Old World a new example. One can see the same trend in something that is as genuinely American as the film industry. There standardization has been employed in the service of individualization. America has been a center of expansion, both for the one and for the other.

A trend towards standardization of quite a different and much more dangerous kind came in the twentieth century from another direction—the Soviet Union of Russia. Here a new communism had gained power and won support in many parts of the world. Dreams of a communistic society where all should be brothers and share alike are both ancient and widespread. They have had their natural soil in basic feelings of good will and neighborly love. We know them from old and new Christian movements, as well as from humanistic plans of brotherhood.

The communism that came to power in the Russian revolution had its theoretical basis in Marxism. These revolutionaries had as their goal a revolution in all the countries of the world. Marxist philosophy has been the starting point of all socialistic conflicts and movements throughout the last one hundred years. It has given unity to the labor movements of the world by creating a common ideology that held the working classes together.[50] This was the doctrine of the class struggle as a major force in social development. One feature of this doctrine was that socialism should be established by a "dictatorship of the proletariat." The Russian Communists reinterpreted this to mean a dictatorship of the party: those who did not belong to the party or accept its leadership would have no rights in society. Everything was to be uniformed according to the orders of the party.

This was directly opposed to the kind of socialism that called itself Social Democratic. The Social Democrats wished to rally the people behind their program. Nevertheless, the revolution in Russia immediately stirred up enthusiasm and sympathy among socialists around the world. It gave them the hope that they too might soon gain their goal. When it became evident that the Russians intended to maintain a permanent dictatorship of the party, more and more of the socialists withdrew.

Neo-Communism nevertheless remained a world movement with supporters in many countries. It could still appeal to social idealism and to an old sympathy with the idea of class conflict. It gained no great strength except in countries where the socialistic labor movement had not been able to project its ideas into an effective social policy, for example, in France and Italy. Then Communism became the program of a revolutionary movement in China, one of the most proletarized countries in the world. It fitted the social conditions there almost better than in Russia. There was no middle ground between the dominant upper class and the workers.

In this way Communism has become a world force and has stirred a worldwide conflict which has affected the philosophy and politics of every country. Virtually all aspects of cultural life have been colored by the struggle. One reason is that the new Communism has demanded standardization even in art and science, a flagrant violation of the spirit of freedom, the vital force in all human progress.

The ideal of freedom received its most complete formulation in the nineteenth century and won its victory in country after country. Freedom included both personal and national liberty, and it was meant to apply equally to all human beings. For a long time it was only the peoples of Europe and the descendants of Europeans who took part in the struggle for freedom. Beyond them and around them lived a whole world of people who did not enjoy any part of it—the peoples of Asia and Africa. In the twentieth century they too began to assimilate the ideal of freedom and promptly turned it against their old European masters. The Arabs who once had been united in a single empire wanted to restore it once more. The Indians, who had never been united until they fell under British domination, began to call for national independence. In this new struggle for freedom religious circumstances were crucial both for union and division. The reason may have been that these new nations had little else to unite them besides religion, which lent the struggle a particularly bitter tone. New burning questions came to the fore. The problem was how one could prevent the liberation of non-European peoples from becoming an enduring rift and a destructive struggle between them and the Europeans.

It is characteristic of the European-American spirit of liberty that the measures adopted by white people in South Africa to keep the colored people in subjection were generally condemned by public opinion in Europe and America. In general, the old colonial powers had given up their dominance of their own free will. There was a widespread desire to assist these once oppressed nations in their efforts to gain better conditions of life, intellectually as well as economically. Rivalry between Communist and non-Communist countries could arise through such a program, but its major feature was an understanding of the bonds that united the entire world.

I wrote my book about American influence in Europe in the years when World War II was approaching its conclusion. At the end of the book I pointed out that the vigorously independent growth of American culture had brought America and Europe so close together that from now on the problem would be one of cooperation rather than of mutual influence. Their oneness is reflected in all possible fields, but perhaps most clearly in scientific work.

A many-faceted cooperation by scientists on both sides of the Atlantic made possible the greatest discovery ever made by man, which made available the enormous power of atomic fission. This new power leaves us with only one alternative—either to give men the possibilities of eternal life on earth, or to destroy the entire human race at a single blow.

The world has never been faced with a more burning question. Have we learned to cooperate? Or shall we go down to destruction together? Can we really comfort ourselves by asking, "Is there any man who dares to take the responsibility for loosing the new forces of destruction?" The responsibility rests upon all of us and the question is whether mutual helpfulness and good will among men are going to grow and develop. There is at least one trend in history that points in this direction.

Chapter XII

INTERNATIONALISM

Although the Greeks were keenly conscious of the opposition between themselves and the barbarians around them, their philosophers bodied forth a lofty vision of the worldwide unity of all men. This was only a dream, however, entertained by a few solitary thinkers. In the early period most people did not look beyond their own borders, and they reckoned only with their own people.

Phoenician voyages of discovery, Greek colonization, and Roman conquests expanded the horizon and gradually welded all the peoples around the Mediterranean into a political and cultural unity. Goods were exchanged between East and West; for example, to a great extent the citizens of Rome lived on grain from Egypt. People could rejoice at a condition of peace that enabled them to travel freely great distances by land and by sea. But no matter how large this world was, it was still surrounded on all sides by enemies it had reason to fear and from whom it had to protect itself by building walls. Individual philosophers might include these enemies in their thoughts of a united humanity, but most people were aware only of their hostility.

The Roman Empire was destroyed by force. One bond,

however, remained and could save at least some of the old unity. This was the Christian religion. When ancient Greece was divided into many independent states, a common religion had helped to create some organization of justice among them, so that their conflicts could be settled by peaceful means, through legal judgments. Even when the Roman Empire was split up, and new European states came into being, Christianity could still promote a certain fellow-feeling between the various nations. In one of the old Articles of Faith the Christians acknowledged their belief in a "Holy Universal Church."

Throughout the Middle Ages the Pope in Rome and the Patriarch in Constantinople each maintained his claim of representing the unity of all churches in the various states. The Christian tradition of peace lived under the surface as a need of the people. It found expression in revolts against the official church, in heretical rebellions that wanted to return the church to its true original Christianity. These religious movements went hand in hand with the rise to power of the middle class.[51] People who lived by trade naturally wanted peace so they could carry on their exchange of goods. At one of the first meetings of the French estates in the fourteenth century, the representative of the citizens, the lawyer Pierre Dubois, proposed a program of peace among all Catholic peoples. He called on them to settle all conflicts by legal means, and he demanded that the Pope should call a general church council to create an international court.

He was ahead of his time in proposing so magnificent a program. Nevertheless the last centuries of the Middle Ages did bring with them an extensive growth of legal procedure. Both in southern Europe, especially the cities of Catalonia, and in the North, especially the cities of the Hanseatic League, rules were established for international trade. These were the beginnings of general international law. Treaties of commerce were drawn up; for example, Norway got its first treaty with the Hanseatic city of Lübeck around 1250. International courts were used in many cases, as between Norway and the Hanseatic cities in 1285. These were often confirmed by treaties declared to be "ever-lasting."

This growth of international law was largely limited to the Catholic countries of western Europe, which is the reason for Dubois' proposal that the Pope should take the lead in working for peace. Dubois' own king vetoed this proposal because he did not wish to strengthen the power of the Pope. The ideal of cooperation nevertheless continued to grow and was strengthened by the need for defending Christendom against the Turkish advances in the East. It was not until the Turks had captured Constantinople that the idea became practical politics. The king of the Czechs, George of Poděbrad (1420–1471), who was an old Hussite, cooperated with a French industrialist, Antonius Marini, in presenting the other western European heads of state with a plan for a union of brotherhood among the Christian states. Above all they were to help one another against the Turks. But they should also have a permanent legal system with a court of arbitration and a mutual agreement to proceed against those who broke the peace.

Fear of the Turks could help to unite the Christians even when they disagreed on religious questions. When the capital of Catholic Germany was threatened by the Turks, the Protestant leader Martin Luther himself gave expression to a common fear and a common will to resistance by writing the hymn "A Mighty Fortress is Our God." It was not easy, however, for the Christian rulers to agree. Each one was thinking of his national interests, and the plan from George of Poděbrad won no support.

A tragic aspect of the rise to power by the middle class was that the citizens were unable to destroy the rule of the nobles in any way other than by supporting an absolute monarchy. This monarchy then became the instrument of a one-sided, nationalistic power politics, with mercantilism as its inevitable partner in economic life.

In spite of all the religious and political cleavage that ushered in the modern period in Europe, the idea of a unity among peoples still remained alive, and it could even gain new strength.

For one thing, the Renaissance saw the rise of a circle of secular intellectuals, the humanists, who came from the ranks of the citizens. These were not bound by the barriers of nation or church, but were joined to others like them by their scientific and cultural interests. The human intellect was to them more important than anything else. They found that war was both stupid and immoral. They believed and taught that all men belonged together and should work together. If they could not abolish war, they could at least build up a system of laws for international relations in war and peace, an international law that the national rulers would be compelled to obey.

At this very time the world expanded by the great over-seas discoveries, which opened up new countries in the West and made the legendary old countries of the East into living realities. Now at last the whole globe came within human purview. The white peoples of Europe saw themselves surrounded by black, yellow, and red races. All the old economic, political, and intellectual problems gained a wider perspective than ever before. People had to learn to think globally. Utopias, or plans for international law, could now embrace all peoples, not just Catholics, or Europeans.

The work of the humanists was brought to fruition by

their successors, the men of the Enlightenment of the eighteenth century. The "Plan for Eternal Peace" that the French abbot St. Pierre prepared in 1713 was in truth a world plan. It became the great program for all European idealists, discussed from Italy to Norway (we are told that our historian Gerhard Schøning believed in it).

If men were to join in such a kingdom of peace, it was necessary that they should understand one another. Neither Latin nor French would suffice; there had to be a universal world language. Philosophers went to work on the problem, particularly the two mathematical philosophers Descartes and Leibniz. They imagined that it might be possible to use a kind of mathematical language, a linguistic algebra, with symbols which each people could pronounce in its own way. This would then be only a written language. Others thought of creating a common spoken language. From the middle of the seventeenth century one proposal after another was made for such a world language. All of them were much too difficult, for they were deliberately constructed without a basis in any living language, lest the various nations should be jealous of one another. Such languages could not gain a foothold among the people, and they remained merely testimonials to the desire for international cooperation.[52] Later centuries have brought forth proposals for interlanguages built more on the living languages of culture. Even they have not become the kind of unifying force that might have been expected.

The many world wars of the eighteenth century were in sharp contrast to the idealism of the period. But the wars were also, in their way, an expression of the new possibilities for global politics. These wars were not just carried on among the great powers of Europe, but also in and for the colonial countries in other parts of the world. They were so many struggles for mastery of the world. Neutral countries were drawn into these wars because they were forced to defend their neutrality. The whole world seemed to be on fire, and people in all countries had reason to tremble at the prospect.

In the midst of this fear the dreams of the utopian idealists were strongly reinforced by the movements for freedom in America and France. From the French Revolution they derived the program of liberty, equality, and fraternity for all men. Even the bloody Napoleonic Wars could not destroy all hope. They rather taught people to face the hard realities. At this very time Immanuel Kant wrote his book *To Eternal Peace*, which maintained that only a union of democratic states could establish lasting peace.[53] Societies that made it their purpose to work for world peace were organized in America and England. At the start they had a purely religious inspiration, a desire to apply Christian principles to world affairs. But they soon won a following among people with purely political motives, and thereby became the focus of an agitation with practical goals.

The nineteenth century has been given various names by historians, most often perhaps "the century of nationalism." One could just as well call it the century of *internationalism*, for the latter movement actually came into being in that century and had a very deep effect on its history.

Czar Alexander I was motivated by a mixture of religious mysticism and reactionary politics when he proposed the Holy Alliance as a union of all European monarchs. The very fact that it was built on power politics made it impossible for him to keep it together for very long. There was much more of a real future in the Young Europe that the Italian revolutionary Mazzini wished to make into an organization for all the democrats of Europe. He too had a program of internationalism. One could say that he wanted to realize in practice the political philosophy of Kant—a union of states on a democratic basis. This goal he could reach only through revolution, and so he organized branches of Young Europe in various countries. The most important of these were Young Italy and Young Germany. Young Europe never became a very strong organization, but it was a source of unrest, particularly in the 1830's, and its agitation reached far and wide. In Norway it influenced the liberal political leader Johan Sverdrup, who jestingly used to call himself "The Young Europe."

It was generally true that revolutionary movements had greater power to arouse worldwide sympathy than the official, conservative propaganda. The Spanish uprising against Napoleon won enthusiastic support in Germany, and also in Norway. The Greek struggle for freedom in 1821 stimulated a general philhellenism that found one spokesman in the Norwegian poet Henrik Wergeland and another in the English poet Byron. After Greece the great symbol for friends of freedom throughout the world was Poland. Later the Hungarian Kossuth and the Italian Garibaldi could become heroes of freedom for all the world. The characteristic feature of the two nineteenth-century revolutions, the July Revolution of 1830 and the February Revolution of 1848, was that they were not confined to a single country, but won wide support and gave birth to a general feeling of unity among all who were battling for political progress.

The work for peace, the very idea of an international order of law, naturally benefited greatly from this new spirit. It is a testimonial to its growth that American friends of peace crossed over to England and organized the first international peace congress in London in 1843. A blacksmith from Connecticut, Elihu Burritt, became a leader in the international peace movement. Beginning in 1847 he organized a whole series of such peace congresses, much larger than the first, in various European capitals. He was the first international journalist in the world, and he made himself into what Americans now call a "columnist." He got space in a number of European newspapers, from Spain to Norway, for his "Olive Leaves," articles about the cause of peace. He gave his thoughts on the subject of peace a more firmly organized form, which included above all an international court. At the congress in Paris in 1849, Victor Hugo launched the slogan of a United States of Europe to stand side by side with the American one. In this connection a demand was launched for free trade among all the countries of Europe. It was an economic internationalism, which wanted to replace both mercantilism and colonialism.

The peace congresses were not the first world congresses. The first peace congress was held in connection with a congress that had already been called for the purpose of united action against Negro slavery, in other words an anti-slavery congress. Before Burritt started his peace congresses, he had taken part in an international temperance congress in London in 1846. All of these congresses were inspired by moral purposes. In this decade the spirit of internationalism began to find expression in congresses held in various other fields as well—politics, economics, science, and other topics of universal interest. Before this time the world had known only congresses of the great powers, which generally had as their purpose to repress all popular movements. Now it was the peoples themselves, or their cultural leaders, who wished to unite for the support of progress and culture. Such congresses were characteristic of the second half of the nineteenth century and continued increasingly in the twentieth.

It is clear that economic, political, moral, and intellectual motives all helped to promote the movement for international cooperation. In so doing they made internationalism itself into a driving force in such activities. People of many professions were infused with an international spirit, so that each of them felt that his work found fulfillment only in an international context. They derived new strength from a union that was as worldwide as possible.

On the political scene the great powers dominated the world more than ever before. They too were carrying on international politics to the extent that they were rivals for world power. Such rivalry did not lead to world peace, but rather filled the world with conflict and strife, which grew more intense as new powers appeared on the scene.

The first attempt to set up a counterweight to the great powers came from the labor movement. This was the organization by socialist workers of the First International in London in 1864. The stimulus to this organization was a meeting a year earlier, held to gain support for the Polish revolt against Russia, the worst of the great powers. This clearly shows that the International was organized primarily to combat the great powers. French and English workmen took the initiative. While the spiritual father of the movement was Karl Marx, the most active propagandist was the Russian Michael Bakunin. His revolutionary agitation frightened authorities in all countries and convinced them that the International was much stronger and more dangerous than it actually was. The organization was soon torn by the conflict between Marx and Bakunin and had to be dissolved.

A new effort was made in 1889, the centennial year of the French Revolution, when the Second International was founded at a labor congress in Paris. This one did become a world organization, with much more strength than the first. Its purpose was to unite the laborers for economic betterment, and there was no such terror connected with it as with the first. It did have political goals, however, primarily that of preventing war between the great powers. In the early years of the twentieth century, with the growing threat of war, the governments of the great powers pretended to respect the wishes of the labor movement with regard to war. The International threatened general revolution if war should be unleashed. It proved to be of no avail. The International suffered a tragic defeat when it was unable to check the World War in 1914.

A Third International was founded by the Russian Communists after they had taken over the power in their country in the Revolution of 1917. The doctrinaire policy of dictatorship that they wanted to force upon the labor movement repelled all democratic workers. Therefore this Third International could not become a truly worldwide force, not even after it had taken over China, the most populous country in the world. The world was now split on a new basis into two opposing power blocs.

The lesson that all socialists had to learn from the defeat of 1914 and the Russian events of 1917 was that it did no good to set up organizations that were separate from or opposed to the rulers of the state. Only through the states could one proceed toward world union. This realization made it possible for socialists to cooperate with other democratic forces in the world. The friends of peace returned to the program Kant had proposed: a union of democratic states as the only basis of lasting world peace.

There was one great power which for the most part had stayed outside the race for world domination. This was the greatest democracy of all, the United States of America. Its president, Woodrow Wilson, stipulated as part of the peace treaty of 1919 that a union of states should be founded for the protection of peace and democracy. The League of Nations was an organization of states, and the representatives who met at its sessions were selected by their governments.

Unfortunately, Wilson was deserted by his own nation, so that the United States did not join. Russia was excluded from the beginning, and about the time it was admitted, Germany withdrew. Nevertheless, this League of Nations was a world union on a great scale, and it became the focus of all work for peace in the world. It did not have the strength, however, to repress the egotism of states and competition among the great powers. The Germany that had left the League at the behest of its dictator Hitler made inflexible demands for more power and thereby initiated a new world war in 1939.

Once more the United States of America interfered decisively in the war. President Franklin D. Roosevelt, a man who himself had served under Wilson, and who came to power early in 1933, at about the same time as Hitler in Germany, threw the entire strength of his country behind the struggle for democracy and world peace. As early as January 1, 1942, he succeeded in getting all the governments that were fighting against Hitler to sign a new declaration of human rights, a proclamation of the freedoms that all of them would try to establish. He succeeded in laying the foundation of a new world organization, the United Nations, which would try to build world peace on a firmer foundation than had the previous League of Nations.

The slogan "One World" was created by his rival for the presidency in 1940, Wendell Willkie, after Roosevelt in 1943 had sent him on a flight around the world to the new powers of Asia. On this flight he learned that no state can isolate itself, that all are indissolubly connected and have to stand together like good brothers.

This is something we have all learned, even though some of us do not yet live by it. It has found a characteristic expression in the help that is being given to underdeveloped peoples, to enable them to reach economic, social, and cultural equality with other nations. In this way one can hope to build a universal sense of brotherhood that will be the best protection for world peace. This is internationalism at its best.

Chapter XIII

CONCLUSION

My purpose in this book has been to discuss, chapter by chapter, all the forces that in one way or another can gain mastery over the human will. I have not attempted to build any systems in this discussion. There are pertinent topics that I have not exhausted. I have only wanted to give some examples to illustrate the effects of certain basic forces in social life. I have included not only *primary* forces, those that are constantly present in human psychology, but also *secondary* forces, which have arisen as a result of historical development.

The sum of all the human wills that have been set in motion in this way is the dynamic that has made history. Only a few of these wills have set themselves goals that extended beyond the day or their immediate circle of acquaintances. Even so, they have all helped to give something. Even if they did no more than work for their own living, they and their beliefs and their wishes were a link in the social structure to which they belonged.

There have always been individuals whose thoughts ranged beyond the day and who wished to impose their ideas on society. Some of them were able to gain power and compel obedience from others. Some had so much spiritual force that others voluntarily accepted their ideas and goals. Still others made inventions that created new conditions of life. These were the statesmen, the scientists, the inventors, and the many others who helped to shape, or to reshape economic, political, and cultural life.

A considerable portion of my own research has consisted in studying the lives and deeds of such exceptional persons. I have written biographies of Henrik Wergeland, Bismarck, Johan Sverdrup, Henrik Ibsen, and many others. Even when I was writing about great general movements like the labor movement, or the agrarian movement in Norway, I have seen fit to embody them in a gallery of individual personalities.

It has not been a part of the plan of this book to include a special discussion of the role such individuals have played in history. If I were to illustrate it with actual examples, there would be too many quite disparate events to set up beside one another. A mathematician contributes something very different to the development of his society than does a statesman, a technologist something different than a poet. All of them, no matter how great their abilities or how strong their wills, have a specific background, in the past and in the present. They do not fall like bombshells on society. No matter how many new things they bring with them, they are all part of a historical context.

One can say the same thing about the various ideas that have been able to gain power over men. I have spoken in the preceding chapters about many such ideas—religious, moral, or political concepts of freedom and cooperation in their various forms. There is a school of historians, with Leopold Ranke as its leader, which maintains that ideas of this kind have dominated history. I have not been able to accept this doctrine, because I have always tried to bring the ideas into connection with real conditions, economic, social, or political. One can not tear ideas loose from the societies in which they arise and are perpetuated. Any such attempt makes it impossible to explain the influence they have been able to exert.

In general I can not make myself believe that the events of history have been determined by any one type of force. It seems clear to me that social development has gradually brought forth more and more forces, spiritual as well as material, that have helped to advance people and groups of people on their paths. Everything that the past has created is part of the life and deed of our day. For this reason all social life has grown ever more complex and intertwined. There are many more wills and interests that now compete for power. The individual, be he politician or labor leader, capitalist or engineer, scientist or artist, can express his personal abilities and purposes in a far more effective way than before. The interplay of abilities has grown richer, and man has more than ever made himself a master of circumstance.

Time and again in our day historians and social thinkers have maintained that the day is past for "great men." Democracy, they say, leaves them no room. Nevertheless, "great men" have arisen, and we need not believe that after this there will be no more of them. One reason for such prophecies is that so much of our political and social life is based on organizations, just as in science there is increasing teamwork. This only means that it takes unusual abilities to rise above the crowd of competent workers. When the general social and cultural level has grown much higher than before, the individual peaks will not perhaps tower as high. Of this, however, we can know nothing. Only the future will show whether it is true.

Our own day has created many new possibilities for

growth and development. A historian must take his lessons from these and become neither dogmatic nor deterministic. Recent English historians have suggested that in every period there are conflicting tendencies, so that at any given moment it may seem possible for historical development to be moving in different directions, giving history a choice. Only later will it be possible to say which trend was the strongest, or, in the usual formulation, was destined to win. An individual can say both "I will" and "I must" at the same time. But when many wills conflict, it is not always easy to say what *must* happen. Historians are therefore growing less confident in their predictions. The events of history have become less and less mechanical, as life has become more complex.

This development, which seems clear in our own time, must have its influence on our view of the past as well. A historian cannot commit himself to any one-sided theory. His pleasure is won from watching all the various forces of history unfold in human society. This may help him to build a coherent philosophy of life for himself. Perhaps it can help others to do the same.

NOTES · INDEX

NOTES

1. "Førebuing til norsk politikk," *Historiske Afhandlinger tilegnet Prof. dr. J. E. Sars* (Christiania, 1905), pp. 132–163.

2. "Genesis of American Independence," *Kristiania Videnskabselskabs Forhandlinger*, no. 3 (1910), 23 pp.

3. See Richard Glover, "Arms and the British Diplomat in the French Revolutionary Era," *Journal of Modern History*, 29:199–212 (1957).

4. Lecture (1913) printed as "Sagaenes opfatning av vår gamle historie," in my book, *Innhogg og utsyn i norsk historie* (Christiania, 1915), pp. 76–91.

5. They are printed in the great collection by J. Mansi, *Sacrorum conciliorum collectio*, 31 folio vols. (Florence, 1759–1798).

6. I wrote a special paper on this topic in 1931, "Kyrke-kløyvinga i Vest-Europa," reprinted in *På leit etter liner i historia* (Oslo, 1953), pp. 145–159; it is based on an earlier paper from 1917.

7. *Die protestantische Ethik und der Geist des Kapitalismus*, first published in *Archiv für Sozialwissenschaft und Sozialpolitik* (1904–1905).

8. "De germanske Folks Samfunds- og Aandsutvikling indtil Lensvæsenets Seier," in *Verdenskulturen*, vol. 3 (Copenhagen, 1907).

9. See my paper, "Den gamle norske rettsstaten," in my book, *Fra norsk midalder* (Bergen, 1959), pp. 27–49.

10. I refer the reader to the chapters on Darwinism in Chr. Collin, *Broderskabets religion og den nye livsvidenskab med en hist. belysning av Darwinismen* (Christiania, 1912).

11. "Moderretsspursmaale, serleg hjaa dei gamle germanarne," *Syn og Segn*, 4:65–92 (1898).

12. See especially my paper, "Norsk historie i lys fra ættehistoria" (1938), reprinted in *På leit etter liner i historia* (Oslo, 1953), pp. 69–83.

13. "Kampen om magten i Norge i sagatiden," *Historisk Tidsskrift*, 5th ser., 4:283–319 (1920), reprinted in *Innhogg og utsyn i norsk historie* (Christiania, 1921), pp. 92–123.

14. "Norsk politisk historie i fyrrhistorisk tid," in my book, *Innhogg og utsyn i norsk historie* (Christiania, 1921), pp. 1–19.

15. In university lectures, later printed in *Verdenskulturen*, vol. 3 (Copenhagen, 1907).

16. See, for example, my book, *Kong Sverre* (Oslo, 1952).

17. "Det nye i norderlendsk historie kringom år 1300," *Scandia*, 4:171–183 (1931), reprinted in *På leit etter liner i historia* (Oslo, 1953), pp. 84–95.

18. "The Dawn of Nationalism in Europe," *American Historical Review*, 52:265–280 (1946–1947); Norwegian trans. in *På leit etter liner i historia* (Oslo, 1953), pp. 52–68.

19. I sketched this development in a lecture on "Nationalism," printed in *Bulletin of the Polish Institute of Arts and Sciences in America*, 3:614–621 (1945).

20. See my opening address at the International Congress of Historians in Oslo (1928), "L'esprit national et l'idée de la souveraineté du peuple," printed in *Bulletin of the International Committee of Historical Sciences*, 2.2:217–224 (Paris, 1929).

21. On this development, see my paper given at the International Congress of Historians in Paris (1950), "Essai sur l'étude de l'histoire du sentiment national," printed in *Avhandlinger utgitt av det Norske Videnskaps-Akademi i Oslo II: 1951*, no. 1.

22. "Upphavet til Renæssansen," *Samtiden*, 33:238–250 (1922).

23. Most recently in the book, *På leit etter liner i historia* (Oslo, 1953), pp. 105–123.

24. "Opphavet til dei store oppfinningane" (1934), first printed in *På leit etter liner i historia* (Oslo, 1953), pp. 160–174.

25. I am here following largely a paper by the American historian Rondo E. Cameron, "Economic Growth and Stagnation in France," *Journal of Modern History*, 30:1–13 (1958).

26. See my lecture on "Det nye i nordisk historie kringom år 1300," delivered at the Scandinavian Historical Congress at Helsinki in 1931, most recently printed in *På leit etter liner i historia* (Oslo, 1953), pp. 84–95.

27. See my book, *Dronning Margareta og Kalmar-unionen* (Oslo, 1956).

28. See my lecture at the International Congress of Historians in Warsaw in 1933, first printed in German in Alfons Dopsch, *Wirtschaft und Kultur* (Vienna, 1938), later in Norwegian as "Statsunionar i sein-midalderen" in *På leit etter liner i historia* (Oslo, 1953), pp. 96–104.

29. See my paper on "Self-assertion of the Farming Class," in *Mélanges d'histoire offerts à Henri Pirenne* (Brussels, 1926), pp. 271–278.

30. *Norsk Bondereising. Fyrebuing til bondepolitikken* (Oslo, 1926), 379 pp.

31. "Førebuing til norsk politikk," *Historiske Afhandlinger tilegnet Prof. dr. J. E. Sars* (Christiania, 1905), pp. 132–163.

32. See my lecture on "Prisar og politikk i norsk historie," given at the Norwegian Historical Meeting in 1912, printed in *Samtiden*, 24:234–252 (1913).

33. See my books, *Socialdemokratie, historisk yversyn* (Christiania, 1915) and *Revolusjonsåret 1848* (Oslo, 1948).

34. See my book, *Arbeiderrørsla av 1848 i Norig* (Christiania, 1914), first printed in German in *Archiv für die Geschichte des Sozialismus und der Arbeiterbewegung*, II (1912).

35. So in my lecture on agrarian politics, "Bondepolitikken," printed in *Samtiden*, 19:437–452 (1908).

36. "The Importance of the Class Struggle in Modern History," *Journal of Modern History*, 1:353–360 (1929), and 2:61–64 (1930).

37. See my paper, "Germansk og romansk," *Syn og Segn*, 24:241–249 (1918).

38. See my lecture of 1910, "Unionssprenginga i 1814 i verdshistorisk samanheng," printed in *På leit etter liner i historia* (Oslo, 1953), pp. 175–187.

39. See my paper, "The Genesis of American Independence" (1910), and my book, *Den amerikanske nasjonen i upphav og reising* (Christiania, 1920).

40. "The Revolutionary Mentality in France, 1793–1794," *History*, 42:181–196 (1957).

41. For more, see my book, *Revolusjons-året 1848* (Oslo, 1948).

42. See my paper, "Den gamle norske rettsstaten," in my book, *Frå norsk midalder* (Bergen, 1959), pp. 27–49.

43. See my paper, "Sættargjerda i Tønsberg 1277," in *Innhogg og utsyn* (Christiania, 1921), pp. 259–272, and "Noreg eit len av St. Olav," in *Historisk Tidsskrift*, 30:81–109 (1934).

44. See my paper, "Luthersk reformasjon og nasjonal frigjøring," *Syn og Segn*, 23:385–398 (1917), and "Kyrke-kløyvinga i Vest-Europa," in *På leit etter liner i historia* (Oslo, 1953), pp. 45–59.

45. In the autumn of 1914 I gave a lecture on "War in World History," printed in *Syn og Segn*, 20:385–394 (1914), as "Krig og framgang." The article gave little of what the title promised.

46. See my paper given at the International Congress of Historians in Paris (1950), "Essai sur l'étude de l'histoire du sentiment national," printed in *Avhandlinger utgitt av det Norske Videnskaps-Akademi i Oslo II: 1951*, no. 1.

47. See my paper, "Peder Claussøns Snorre som norsk bondelesning," *Historisk Tidsskrift*, 5th ser., 5:102–113 (1921), and others in the same volume.

48. "Historieskriving og folkevokster," in *Norsk Historisk Videnskap i Femti År, 1869–1919* (Christiania, 1920), pp. 1–18.

49. *The American Spirit in Europe* (Philadelphia, 1949), 289 pp.

50. See my book, *Socialdemokratie* (Christiania, 1915; new ed., Oslo, 1932).

51. See my article, "Fram til Folkenes Forbund," *Tidens Tegn* (Christiania), Dec. 29, 1919; this was written apropos of Chr. L. Lange, *Histoire de l'internationalisme*, vol. 1 (Christiania, 1919), but was also based on independent research.

52. See my article, "Samfolkelegt hjelpemaal—kunstigt eller naturlegt," *Syn og Segn*, 18:1–15, 65–77 (1912).

53. Immanuel Kant, *Zum ewigen Frieden* (1795).

INDEX

Aall, Jacob, 168
Abelard, Pierre, 166
Absalon, archbishop of Lund, 76
Adams, Henry, 9, 21
Africa, 84, 100, 151, 156, 186–187
Aggressive tendencies, 18, 59, 77, 153–154, 157
Agrarian movement, 115–120
Agriculture, 176
Airplanes, 162
Albigensians, 46
Alexander I, czar of Russia, 194
Alexander the Great, 75
Allah, 39
Alsace-Lorraine, 155
America, *see* United States
American Revolution, 28, 131–133, 181–182
Americanization, 183–184, 187
Angell, Norman: *The Great Illusion*, 158
Animals, domestic, 176
Arabs, 156, 180, 187
Aristotle, 34, 165–166
Armaments, 158, 161–162
Arminius, 167
Arthur, King, 72, 108
Arup, Erik, 84
Aschehoug, T. H., 169, 171

Ashley, William, 87
Asia, 145, 151, 186
Asia Minor, 176
Associations, 146–147
Assyria, 5, 19, 65
Athenians, 123
Atlanta, Georgia, 93
Atomic fission, 162, 163, 188
Augustine, Saint, 44, 84, 127, 165
Augustus, Roman emperor, 26
Australia, 60
Austria, 79–80, 89, 110
Aztecs, 19

Babylonia, 164–165
Bakunin, Michael, 197
Baltic countries, 159, 160
Beccaria, Cesare, 181
Belgium, 182
Bergen, Norway, 90, 144
Bergen-Oslo railroad, 91–92
Bible, 165, 172
Bill of Rights, 133
Birkeland, Michael, 169, 171
Bismarck, 89–90
Bloch, Johann von, 158
Boccaccio, 95
Bohemia, 110, 111, 159, 169

Bohr, Niels, 21
Boleslav I, king of Poland, 75
Bolin, Sture, 85
Bourgeoisie, 78, 90, 91, 96, 111–113, 134, 146, 181–182, 192
Bruno, Giordano, 172
Brutus, 72
Buckle, Henry Thomas, 2–3
Buddhism, 35–36, 177
Bugge, Sophus, 170
Burgundians, 156
Burritt, Elihu, 195–196
Byron, Lord, 195
Byzantium, 96

Calvin, John, 129, 142
Canada, 132
Capitalism, 16, 31, 52–53, 95–96, 150
Carolingian era, 85–86
Carthage, 20–21
Casimir the Just, 75
Catalonia, 190
Catherine of Siena, Saint, 174
Chance in history, 26–29
Charlemagne, 53–55, 68, 73, 140
Charles V, Holy Roman emperor, 51
China, 5, 19, 20, 151, 155, 165, 180, 186
Christian III, king of Denmark, 49–50
Christianity, 36–38, 40–47, 53–56, 63, 125, 139–142, 156, 177–180, 190–191
Cleopatra, 26
Cobb, Richard, 133–134
Codfish industry, 90–91
Colonialism, 99–101, 157, 187
Communism, 148, 150, 185–186, 187
Communist Manifesto, 106
Comte, Auguste, 14
Condorcet, Marquis de, 12–15
Constantine the Great, 139
Constantinople, 191
Copenhagen, Council of (1660), 112
Copernicus, 171
Copper, 176
Corsica, 62
Crimean War, 160
Cromwell, Oliver, 52
Crusades, 180

Cultural development, see Progress, idea of
Cultural influences, 175–181
Cultures, growth and decline of, 17–22
Cyprus, 19, 176

Daae, Ludwig, 91
Dante, 95
Darwin, Charles, 58, 99, 172; The Descent of Man, 58, 172
Davy, Sir Humphry, 13
Descartes, René, 193
Declaration of Independence, 133
Democracy, 79, 149
Denmark: absolute monarchy, 112–113; agrarianism, 115; bourgeoisie, 112–113; mercantilism, 113; nationalism, 76; nobility, 110, 112; Reformation, 49–50
Dervishes, 7
Dionysius, Saint, 141
Dominican order, 100
Donatello, 95
Don Quixote, 113
Dopsch, Alfons, 85
Dubois, Pierre, 190–191
Dudo, Norman historian, 76

Egypt, 5, 19, 65, 189
Eidsivathing, 65
Eidsvoll, Norway, 136, 168
Einstein, Albert, 18, 164
Eirik, Earl, 77
Elizabeth I, queen of England, 87
Engelbrekt Engelbrektsson, 111
England: feudalism, 68; nationalism, 71–73, 87–88; Puritanism, 52–53, 142–143; Reformation, 48–49; trade, 87; unification, 88, 109; war, 101, 102, 159. See also American Revolution
Enlightenment, age of, 12–13, 97, 193
Erslev, Kristian, 108
Evolution, concept of, 172–173

February Revolution (1848), 195
Feudalism, 66–68, 85–86, 129
Finland, 160
Flanders, 87, 96, 101

Florence, 95–96, 97–98
Folkungs (Swedish royal family), 68, 108
France: agrarianism, 114; church in, 47, 51; communism, 186; heretical movement, 44; Industrial Revolution, 102–103; nationalism, 73–74, 167; population, 103–104; Renaissance, 96–97, 167; unification, 88–89; war, 102, 104. *See also* French Revolution
Franciscans, 94, 100
Franco, Francisco, 158
Franklin, Benjamin, 181
Franks, 156
French Revolution, 12, 13, 29, 71, 104, 114, 117, 120, 125, 134–135, 182, 194
Freud, Sigmund, 3, 37, 61; *Totem and Taboo*, 61
Frostathing, 65, 126

Galileo, 172
Garibaldi, 195
Gaul, 156
Geneva, Switzerland, 142
Geoffrey of Monmouth, 72, 75, 76
Germanic peoples, 51, 60, 84, 128–129
Germany: nationalism, 74, 79; Reformation, 48; religion, 51; Renaissance, 167; trade, 144; unification, 89, 110; war, 156–157, 160, 189; Young Germany, 195
Ghettos, 63
Gibbon, Edward, 13
Gibbs, Josiah Willard, 21, 164
Gjessing, Gutorm: *Man and Culture*, 59
God in history, 25, 124–126
Goethe, 182
Gothic architecture, 98
Goths, 156, 167
Great Britain, *see* England
Greece, 5, 13, 123, 159, 189, 195
Greek philosophy, 166–167, 171
Gregory I (the Great), pope, 42
Gregory VII, pope, 126, 142
Guilds, 16, 95–96, 146
Guizot, Francois, 118, 128–129
Gulathing, 65
Gustavus Adolphus, king of Sweden, 51

Gustavus Vasa, king of Sweden, 49

Haakon I, king of Norway, 65
Halvdan the Black (the Swarthy), 65
Hanseatic League, 89, 91, 101, 190–191
Harald I, the Fairhaired, 62, 69, 130, 138
Harald III, the Stern, 77
Hauge movement, Norway, 46
Hegel, G. W. F., 14
Henri IV, king of France, 128
Henry IV, Holy Roman emperor, 126, 142
Henry VIII, king of England, 48–49
Heretical movements, 43–47, 94, 130, 180
Heritage: cultural, 4–9, 11–12, 19–20, 22; historical, 164; psychological, 2–4, 10–11, 117
Hespriholmen, 59
Hipparchos, 127
Historical research, 29–31, 164, 167–171, 202–204
Hitler, Adolf, 128, 199
Holberg, Ludwig: *Don Ranudo*, 113
Holland, *see* Netherlands, The
Holy Alliance, 194
Homer, 13, 69
Hugo, Victor, 196
Human life, continuity of, 3–9
Human rights, 43, 120, 133, 158, 182, 186
Humanistic sciences, 164
Humanists, 192
Humanitarianism, 56
Hundred Years' War, 101, 110, 145
Hungary, 79–80, 110
Hussites, 46, 111, 159, 180

Iberian peninsula, 110. *See also* Spain.
Ibsen, Henrik, 15, 69, 137, 148; *The Pretenders*, 69
Iceland, 50, 129
Incas, 19
Independence movements, 159–160, 186–187. *See also* American Revolution; Norway, independence
India, 5, 20, 151–152, 165, 180, 187
Indians, American, 60, 100

Individualism, 12–13, 94–96, 99, 128–129
Industrial Revolution, 97–99, 102–103, 118, 183
Innocent III, pope, 75, 142
International law, 190–191, 192
International politics, 101–102, 197
Internationals: First, 197; Second, 197–198; Third, 198
Inventions, 11–12, 18, 97–99, 161–162, 183–184
Iron, 64, 176
Italy: communism, 186; continuity of human life in, 7–9; heretical movement, 44; nationalism, 74–75, 79; Renaissance, 94–96; schools, 143; trade, 144

Japan, 67, 160
Jefferson, Thomas, 182
Jensen, Johannes V., 5; *The Long Journey*, 5
Jessen, Edwin, 170
Jesuits, 100, 143, 151
Jesus, 36–38, 50
Jews, 41, 63
Jordanes, Ostrogothic author, 64
Jorga, Nicolae, 1
July Revolution (1830), 195

Kant, Immanuel, 194–195, 198; *To Eternal Peace*, 194
Kepler, Johannes, 172
Keyser, Rudolf, 169
Kings, 65–70, 78, 80, 111–113, 126–127, 138, 141–142, 194
Kinship, 62–63
Koran, 139
Kossuth, Lajos, 195
Kropotkin, N., 58

Labor movement, 45, 118–122, 125, 147
Lade, earls of, 63
Lamprecht, Karl, 23, 33, 89, 95
Languages: national, 78–79, 145–146, 171, 180; world, 193
Las Casas, Bartolome de, 100
Latin, 145, 180–181

League of Nations, 199
Le Bon, Gustave, 3
Leibniz, Gottfried Wilhelm von, baron, 193
Lessing, Gotthold E., 30
Liberalism, 16, 99, 146
Lithuania, 109
Locke, John, 133
Lofthaus Revolt, 118
Lollards, 46, 47
London, England, 87
Lower classes, 106–107, 110–111, 114–115, 117, 124
Luther, Martin, 47, 48, 129, 191
Lutheranism, 46

McDougall, William, 2, 3, 4; *Introduction to Social Psychology*, 2; *The Group Mind*, 2
Machiavelli, 154
Magna Charta, 88, 127
Magnus, Olaus, 167
Magnus I, the Law-mender, king of Sweden, 55
"Maid from Norway," 109
Malthus, Thomas R., 58
Manicheans, 44
March of the Girondists, 123
Margaret, queen of Denmark, Norway, and Sweden, 47, 108–109
Marini, Antonius, 191
Marx, Karl, 82, 99, 120, 134, 148, 197
Marxism, 82–83, 93–94, 96, 106, 115, 119, 148, 185
Matriarchy, 60–62
Mazzini, Giuseppe, 194
Mecca, 39
Medina, 39
Mercantilism, 16, 78, 88, 111, 113, 143–146, 182, 190
Mexico, 27
Missionaries, 100
Mohammedanism, 38–39, 80, 139, 165, 177, 179–180
Moltke, Helmuth von, 15
Montesquieu, 2, 29, 181
Morality, 34–35, 39, 56, 141, 154–155
Mosaic code, 35, 54, 139

Munch, P. A., 169; *History of the Norwegian People*, 169

Nansen, Hans, 112
Napoleon, 195
National character, 2–3
Nationalism, 70–81, 167–169
Natural conditions and history, 1, 24–26, 83
Natural rights, 79
Natural sciences, 21, 164
Negro slavery, 43, 92, 100, 196
Netherlands, The, 131, 143, 144
Neutrality, 157
Newton, Sir Isaac, 13, 21, 172
Nobility, 27, 62, 63, 107–114, 134
Nordic unity, 64, 108–109
Normandy, 97, 167
Norway: absolute monarchy, 112–113; agrarianism, 115–118, 119; bourgeoisie, 112; Christianity, 55, 178–179; church laws, 40, 43, 55, 126–127; feudalism, 68; historical writings, 168–169; independence, 120–121, 131, 135–136, 169–170, 182; labor movement, 119; migration to Iceland, 129–130; nationalism, 76–77, 168–169, 171; nobility, 27, 62, 112; paganism, 178–179; Reformation, 50; Renaissance, 97, 167; sagas, 64–65, 127, 167, 168–169; school legislation, 125; trade, 144, 191; unification, 64–65, 90–92, 171

Olaf Tryggveson, king of Norway, 77
Olav, Saint, 141
Ostwald, Wilhelm, 24

Palacky, Francis, 169
Parsifal, 108
Pascal, Blaise, 26
Patriarchy, 60–62
Patriotism, 70
Paul, Apostle, 179
Peace movements, 194, 195–196
Peder Clausson, 168
Persia, 67
Peter, Saint, 140
Petrarch, 95

Phidias, 13
Philhellenism, 159, 195
Phoenicia, 19, 189
Pierre of Blois, 73
Pirenne, Henri, 16, 28, 31, 85
Pitt, William, 182
Plato, 13, 165–166
Plebeians, 107
Podebrad, George of, Czech king, 191
Pokrowski, Mikhail, 83
Poland, 51, 75–76, 79, 109, 110, 195, 197
Polybius, 28, 29
Pope, power of, 47, 190–191
Portugal, 47
Power politics, 110, 154–155, 158, 194
Primitive peoples, 4–5, 9–11, 25, 33, 59, 62
Progress, idea of, 13–19, 22–23, 175
Protectionism, 146, 149
Psychoanalysis, 3
Psychology, 173; mass, 2–3, social, 2–4, 137
Punishment, 55–56
Puritanism, 52–53

Quetelet, Lambert, 30

Ranke, Leopold, 30, 202
Ranrike, 64
Rantzau, Henrik, 6
Realism in literature, 173
Reformation, 46–50, 129, 142–143, 180
Religion, 7, 9, 19, 32–57, 177–180
Religious wars, 50–52, 53, 156–157
Renaissance, 15–16, 78, 94–97, 166–167, 192
Revolutionary movements, 148, 158–160, 185–186. *See also* French Revolution.
Revolutions, political, 158, 160, 185–186
Ringerike, 64, 116
Robespierre, 134
Rodulf, early king in Norway, 64
Roland, of the *Song of Roland*, 73
Roman Empire, 13, 18, 26, 67, 71, 128, 155, 177–179, 189–190
Roman literature, 166–167

Romanticism, 71, 79, 108, 128
Romerike, 64
Roosevelt, Franklin D., 150, 199
Rothe, Tyge: *Nordens Statsforfatning* ("Political Constitution of Scandinavia"), 168
Rousseau, Jean Jacques, 181
Russia, 18, 102, 104; Revolution, 148, 160, 185–186

Saint-Pierre, Abbé Charles-Irénée de, 193
Saint-Simon, Comte de, 118
Salamis, 159
Sars, J. E., 140, 169, 170–171
Saxo Grammaticus, Danish historian, 76
Schleswig, 110
Schoning, Gerhard, 193
Schools, secular, 143
Scotland, 62, 109
Septimius Severus, 84
Shakespeare, 15
Shaman, 34
Shays' Rebellion, 118
Sicily, 7, 62, 156, 180
Sieyès, Abbé, 114
Slavery, 40–43. *See also* Negro slavery.
Smith, Adam, 99, 182; *Wealth of Nations*, 99
Snorri Sturluson, 30, 76–77, 126, 130, 168
Social structure, Middle Ages, 111
Social welfare, 146–147
Socialism, 120, 136, 146–147, 185–186
Socrates, 6, 178
Sovereignty of the people, 127
Spain, 47, 100, 110, 156, 158–159, 180
Spartacus, 124
Spartans, 123–124
Spencer, Herbert, 21
Spengler, Oswald, 17–20
Standardization, 184–186
Stone Age, 59, 175–176
Struggle for existence, 5, 58, 83
Suger, abbot of Saint-Denis, 73, 74
Svane Hans, 112
Sven Aggeson, 76
Sverdrup, Johan, 195

Sverre Sigurdsson, king of Norway, 66, 68, 91, 142, 144
Sweden: church in, 49; Dalecarlian uprising, 111; nationalism, 167–168; nobility, 110, 112
Syracuse, 8

Tacitus, 83–84, 128
Temperance Congress, 196
Ten Commandments, 35, 165
Theology, 165–166
Thermopylae, 123, 159
Thierry, Auguste, 118
"Third Estate," 114, 120, 121
Thirty Years' War, 51, 156–157
Thomas Aquinas, 125, 166
Thrane, Marcus, 119
Thucydides, 29
Tithes, 37–38, 141
Tocqueville, Alexis de, 183
Torture, 10
Toynbee, Arnold J., 17–19, 26; *A Study of History*, 17
Trade, 63–64, 65, 86
Traits, basic, *see* Heritage
Tristram, 108
Turkey, 67, 159, 179, 191
Tyrants, 125–128

Ukraine, 121
Underdeveloped peoples, 187, 200
Undset, Sigrid, 174
United Nations, 199
Union of Soviet Socialist Republics, *see* Russia
United States: agrarianism, 117–118; force in world history, 181; New Deal, 150; peace movements, 195–196, 198–199; politics, 149–150; Puritanism, 142–143; technology, 183–185; unification, 92–93. *See also* American Revolution.
Upper classes, 21, 84–85, 106–107

Valdemars, Danish kings, 68
Veblen, Thorstein, 84
Vendettas, 62
Vercingetorix, Gaulish chieftain, 167
Villages, 84

Vincentius, bishop of Cracow, 75
Virgil, 71
Voltaire, 143, 172, 181

Waldemars, *see* Valdemars
Walther von der Vogelweide, 74
War, 15, 64–66, 69, 80, 101–102, 153–162, 192. *See also* Hundred Years' War; Religious wars; Thirty Years' War; Wars of the Roses.
Wars of the Roses, 110
Washington, George, 182
Weber, Max, 52–53
Weibull, Curt, 30
Welfare state, 15, 54
Welshmen, 72

Wergeland, Henrik, 195; *The Result of History*, 13, 20; *Man, Creation and Messiah*, 32
Whale fat, 162
Willkie, Wendell, 199
William the Conqueror, 68
Wilson, Woodrow, 198
Woolen industry, 87, 95
World Congresses: anti-slavery, 196; peace, 195–196; temperance, 196
World wars, 102, 157, 160–162

Ynglings, early rulers of Sweden, 77
Young Europe, 194–195

Zwingli, Ulrich, 48